Praise for *Leadership and Self-Deception*

"This is a profound book, with deep and sweeping implications. I couldn't recommend it more highly."
—Stephen R. Covey, author of *The 7 Habits of Highly Effective People*

"This is the most profound and practical business book I have ever read! Everyone I have recommended this book to has been challenged intellectually and also touched emotionally. It is a must-read that I will give to my kids to read before they begin their careers."
—Tom A. DiDonato, Senior Vice President, Human Resources, Lear Corporation

"I love this book. It identifies the central issue in all organizational performance. Like truth itself, this book reveals more with each re-examination. I highly recommend it."
—Doug Hauth, Business Development Manager, Convio, Inc.

"Imagine working in an organization where the aim of your colleagues is to help you achieve your results. I could not believe it possible. After reading this book I just had to bring Arbinger to the UK to teach our people. What an experience! We are all better people for it. This book touches the very foundation of culture, teamwork, and performance."
—Mark Ashworth, President and CEO, Butcher's Pet Care, UK

"It's rare to find a business book that is good enough to recommend to your boss, your work team, and your friends. The concepts in this book have transformed both the way I work and the way I live."
—Robert W. Edwards, Managing Director, Sales, FedEx

"After decades of executive leadership in senior management positions, I've finally found in Arbinger what I consider to be the best means of improving every measure of success. From boosting the bottom line to increasing personal joy, this book shows the way."
—Bruce L. Christensen, former President and CEO, PBS

"This astonishing book is a MUST-read for every executive or personal and professional coach."
—Laura Whitworth, coauthor of *Co-Active Coaching*, and cofounder, The Coaches Training Institute

"The concepts in this book are powerful. They are fundamental to success whether on the playing field, in the office, or perhaps most importantly, at home. Read this book and you'll see what I mean."
—Steve Young, two-time NFL Most Valuable Player

"Rarely has a book had such an immediate and profound impact on the hundreds of CEOs of fast-growth firms we work with through our MIT/Inc./EO Executive Program. And it's one of those rare books that touches both the personal as well as professional lives of these leaders."
—Verne Harnish, cofounder, Entrepreneurs' Organization, and CEO, Gazelles, Inc.

"*Leadership and Self-Deception* is a touchstone for authentic leadership. Arbinger's innovative exploration of what lies beneath behavior uplifts, enlightens, and transforms. We've wholeheartedly adopted *Leadership and Self-Deception* as the foundational material for our administrator development program."
—Troy S. Buer, Educational Program Director, University of Virginia School of Medicine

"This is probably the most outstanding book that directs us to soul searching and introspection. It teaches us to take accountability for our lives and our destinies in a down-to-earth and bluntly practical manner. The lessons in this book have helped me personally, as well as other people I love."
—Kalyan Banerjee, cofounder and Senior Vice President, MindTree

"The principles of *Leadership and Self-Deception* provide the groundwork for our success as individuals and organizations. I recommend it highly to my fellow board members and to global networks, corporate clients, entrepreneurs, and individuals alike."
—Heidi Forbes Öste, CEO and founder, 2BalanceU, and Public Relations, Europe Region, Business and Professional Women International

"While reading, I reviewed my life, and, sure enough, what successes there were in it were based on Arbinger's principles. This book is a tool that could transform and elevate the way government functions!"
—Mark W. Cannon, former Administrative Assistant to the Chief Justice of the United States, and Staff Director, Commission on the Bicentennial of the US Constitution

"Because it distills important leadership, spiritual, and life principles into one profound and impossible-to-put-down book, *Leadership and Self-Deception* is a treasure. MBA students in my classes share my enthusiasm for this rare book. You will surely return to this book again and again; and each time you do, it will be as penetrating a learning experience as the first time."
—Barry Brownstein, CSX Chair in Leadership, University of Baltimore

"The leadership principles in this book have had a greater impact on the quality of leadership in our company than anything we have ever implemented. They have been extraordinarily important in helping make our company a great place to work while at the same time helping us focus on results and increase productivity as never before."
—Michael Stapley, President and CEO, DMBA

"Simple . . . clear . . . powerful. With many years of experience in leadership, organizational development, and training I was surprised to find something strike me with such impact."
—Janet Steinwedel, President, Leader's Insight

"As a therapist I was pleasantly surprised to find that a book geared toward managers could have such far-reaching implications in my life and the lives of my clients. I believe the ideas in this book could transform the counseling profession. It is now required reading for all my clients."
—Jason Beard, family therapist

"Are you relating to the world anxiously or angrily, not comprehending why you hold judgmental attitudes, feel uncontrollable fear, or unleash explosions of temper against your colleagues without being able to explain why? Do you feel hopeless and unable to change? Learn the practical tools provided in this fascinating book and eliminate this problem at its source right now!"
—Marcos Cajina Heinzkill, Certified Coach and Facilitator, founder and President, Renewal, Spain

"Remarkable. Arbinger possesses the hidden key to productivity and creativity. Do whatever you can to get your hands on this material."
—Dave Browne, former President and CEO, LensCrafters

"This book is a rare gem that is treasured by all who have read it. The organization for which I work has passed this book to so many people, and it is amazing to watch people's attitudes and behaviors toward each other changing. Each day everyone gives a little more, making us better leaders, but more importantly, better people."
—Nuala Murphy, Senior Vice President,
Global Financial Services Company

"*Leadership and Self-Deception* holds up a brutally honest mirror to behavior in which we all indulge to justify our shortcomings. The result is not self-remorse or punishment but a glimpse of a life to be lived with integrity and freed of the boundaries and constraints we inflict upon ourselves and others. I am always excited to watch Arbinger's thinking help my clients to unlock painful family disputes and lead them to resolution."
—Neil Denny, family lawyer, Wiltshire, UK

"A remarkable book. It can be valuable to your understanding of why so many people create their own problems, are unable and/or unwilling to see that they are creating their own problems, and then resist any attempts by others to help them stop creating those problems."
—Robert Morris, Amazon Top 50 Reviewer

"I've been in the book publishing business for twenty-five years. Rarely have I read a book as profound and life-changing as *Leadership and Self-Deception*."
—David Sanford, Literary Agent, Credo Communications

"This book was recommended to me at an annual strategic planning session. I was stunned by the truth of it and the simple solution. Our entire management has now read it. It has been a building block for our personal and organizational development."
—Rick Chalk, CEO, Cal-Tex Protective Coatings

"My business partners and I built a health-care company on the ideas in this book. We are amazed at what it has helped us achieve. Careful reading and rereading of this book has proven better than any productivity, team-building, or leadership training we've encountered."
—Mark Ballif, CEO, Plum Healthcare

LEADERSHIP AND SELF-DECEPTION

Getting Out of the Box

THE ARBINGER INSTITUTE

BK

Berrett–Koehler Publishers, Inc.
a BK Business book

Berrett-Koehler Publishers, Inc.
1333 Broadway, Suite 1000
Oakland, CA 94612-1921
Tel: (510) 817-2277   Fax: (510) 817-2278   www.bkconnection.com

Ordering Information

Quantity sales. Special discounts are available on quantity purchases by corporations, associations, and others. For details, contact the "Special Sales Department" at the Berrett-Koehler address above.

Individual sales. Berrett-Koehler publications are available through most bookstores. They can also be ordered directly from Berrett-Koehler: Tel: (800) 929-2929; Fax: (802) 864-7626; www.bkconnection.com.

Orders for college textbook / course adoption use. Please contact Berrett-Koehler: Tel: (800) 929-2929; Fax: (802) 864-7626.

Distributed to the U.S. trade and internationally by Penguin Random House Publisher Services.

Berrett-Koehler and the BK logo are registered trademarks of Berrett-Koehler Publishers, Inc.

Printed in Canada.

Berrett-Koehler books are printed on long-lasting acid-free paper. When it is available, we choose paper that has been manufactured by environmentally responsible processes. These may include using trees grown in sustainable forests, incorporating recycled paper, minimizing chlorine in bleaching, or recycling the energy produced at the paper mill.

Library of Congress Cataloging-in-Publication Data
Names: Arbinger Institute.
Title: Leadership and self-deception / The Arbinger Institute.
Description: Third Edition. | Oakland, CA : Berrett-Koehler Publishers, 2018. |
   Revised edition of Leadership and self-deception, c2010. | Includes
   bibliographical references and index.
Identifiers: LCCN 2018019155 | ISBN 9781523097807 (paperback)
Subjects: LCSH: Leadership. | Self-deception. | BISAC: BUSINESS &
   ECONOMICS / Leadership. | SELF-HELP / Personal Growth / General. |
   FAMILY & RELATIONSHIPS / Conflict Resolution.
Classification: LCC HD57.7 .L4315 2018 | DDC 658.4/092–dc23
LC record available at https://lccn.loc.gov/2018019155

THIRD EDITION
25 24 23 22 21 20 19 18   12 11 10 9 8 7 6 5 4 3 2 1

Copyediting and proofreading: PeopleSpeak
Production: Marin Bookworks
Interior illustrations and cover design: Michael Brown

"It is in the darkness of their eyes that men get lost."
—Black Elk

Contents

Preface

For too long, the issue of self-deception has been the realm of deep-thinking philosophers, academics, and scholars working on the central questions of the human sciences. The public remains generally unaware of the issue. That would be fine except that self-deception is so pervasive that it touches every aspect of life. "Touches" is perhaps too gentle a word to describe its influence. Self-deception actually *determines* one's experience in every aspect of life. The extent to which it does that—and in particular the extent to which it determines the nature of one's influence on, and experience of, others—is the subject of this book.

To give you an idea of what's at stake, consider the following analogy. An infant is learning how to crawl. She begins by pushing herself backward around the house. Backing herself around, she gets lodged beneath the furniture. There she thrashes about, crying and banging her little head against the sides and undersides of the pieces. She is stuck and hates it. So she does the only thing she can think of to get herself out—she pushes even harder, which only worsens her problem. She's more stuck than ever.

If this infant could talk, she would blame the furniture for her troubles. After all, she is doing everything she can think of. The problem couldn't be *hers*. But of course the problem *is* hers, even though she can't see it. While it's true that she's doing everything she can think of, the problem is precisely that *she can't see how she's the problem*. Having the problem she has, nothing she can think of will be a solution.

Self-deception is like this. It blinds us to the true causes of problems, and once we're blind, all the "solutions" we can think of will actually make matters worse. Whether at work or at home, self-deception obscures the truth about ourselves, corrupts our view of others and our circumstances, and inhibits our ability to make wise and helpful decisions. To the extent that we are self-deceived, both our happiness and our leadership are undermined at every turn, and not because of the furniture.

We have written this book to educate people about a solution to this most central of problems. Our experience in teaching about self-deception and its solution is that people find this knowledge liberating. It sharpens vision, reduces feelings of conflict, enlivens the desire for teamwork, redoubles accountability, magnifies the capacity to achieve results, and deepens satisfaction and happiness. This is true whether we are sharing these ideas with corporate executives in New York, governmental leaders in Beijing, community activists on the West Bank, or parenting groups in Brazil. Members of every culture participate to one degree or another in their own individual and cultural self-deceptions. The discovery of a way out of those self-deceptions is the discovery of hope and the birth of new possibilities and lasting solutions.

This book was first published in 2000. In this new third edition, published in 2018, the text has been updated, and we have added new sections at the end that describe research into the magnitude of self-deception in organizations, how to measure the extent of self-deception in organizations, and various uses people have made of the book and its ideas over the nearly two decades since it was first published.

Initially, some readers are surprised to find that the book unfolds as a story. Although fictional, the characters' experiences are drawn from our own and our clients' actual experiences, so the story rings true, and most readers tell us that they see themselves in it. Because of this, the book delivers not just conceptual but also practical understanding of the problem of self-deception and its solution.

The resulting impact has made *Leadership and Self-Deception* one of the bestselling leadership books of all time. The book's sequel, *The Anatomy of Peace*, originally published in 2006, builds on both the story and the ideas developed in *Leadership and Self-Deception*. It has occupied the number one position on the bestseller lists in the categories of War and Peace and Conflict Resolution for over a decade. Our most recent bestseller, *The Outward Mindset*, shows how organizations can successfully implement the ideas first introduced in *Leadership and Self-Deception*. Individually and together, these books help readers to see their work lives and home situations in entirely new ways and to discover practical and powerful solutions to problems they were sure were someone else's.

We couldn't have foreseen what would happen with *Leadership and Self-Deception*. Few people had ever heard of the Arbinger Institute when the book was first published, and our choice to publish in the name of the company bucked industry norms. But the book blazed a trail. It is now an enduring classic with a message as important and relevant as ever. We are confident that this introduction to the self-deception problem and solution will give you new and helpful leverage both personally and professionally—leverage to see yourself, others, and your challenges differently, and to solve problems that have stubbornly resisted solution.

PART I

Self-Deception and the "Box"

1 *Bud*

It was a brilliant summer morning shortly before nine, and I was hurrying to the most important meeting of my new job at Zagrum Company. As I walked across the tree-lined grounds, I recalled the day two months earlier when I had first entered the secluded campus-style headquarters to interview for a senior management position. I had been watching the company for more than a decade from my perch at one of its competitors and had tired of finishing second. After eight interviews and three weeks spent doubting myself and waiting for news, I was hired to lead one of Zagrum's product lines.

Now, four weeks later, I was about to be introduced to a senior management ritual peculiar to Zagrum: a daylong one-on-one meeting with the executive vice president, Bud Jefferson. Bud was the right-hand man to Zagrum's president, Kate Stenarude. And due to a shift within the executive team, he was about to become my new boss.

I had tried to find out what this meeting was all about, but my colleagues' explanations confused me. They mentioned a discovery that solves "people problems"; how no one really focuses on results; and that something about the "Bud Meeting," as it was called, and strategies that evidently follow from it, are key to Zagrum's incredible success. I had no idea what they were talking about, but I was eager to meet, and impress, my new boss.

Bud Jefferson was a youngish-looking 50-year-old combination of odd-fitting characteristics: a wealthy man who drove around in an economy car without hubcaps; a near–high school dropout with law and business degrees, summa cum laude, from Harvard; a connoisseur of the arts who was hooked on the Beatles. Despite his apparent contradictions, and perhaps partly because of them, Bud was revered as something of an icon. He was universally admired in the company.

It took 12 minutes on foot to cover the distance from my office in Building 8 to the lobby of the Central Building. The pathway—one of many connecting Zagrum's 10 buildings—meandered beneath oak and maple canopies along the banks of Kate's Creek, a postcard-perfect stream that was the brainchild of Kate Stenarude and had been named after her by the employees.

As I scaled the Central Building's hanging steel stairway up to the third floor, I reviewed my performance during my month at Zagrum: I was always among the earliest to arrive and latest to leave. I felt that I was focused and didn't let outside matters interfere with my objectives. Although my wife often complained about it, I was making a point to outwork and outshine every coworker who might compete for promotions in the coming years. I nodded to myself in satisfaction. I had nothing to be ashamed of. I was ready to meet Bud Jefferson.

Arriving in the main lobby of the third floor, I was greeted by Bud's secretary, Maria. "You must be Tom Callum," she said with enthusiasm.

"Yes, thank you. I have an appointment with Bud for nine o'clock," I said.

"Of course. Bud asked me to have you wait for him in the Eastview Room. He should be with you in about five minutes." Maria escorted me down the hall and into a large conference room. I went to the long bank of windows and admired the views of the campus between the leaves of the green Connecticut woods. A minute or so later, there was a brisk knock on the door, and in walked Bud.

"Hello, Tom. Thanks for coming," he said with a big smile as he offered his hand. "Please, sit down. Can I get you something to drink? Coffee, juice?"

"No, thank you," I replied. "I've had plenty already this morning."

I settled in the black leather chair nearest me, my back to the window, and waited for Bud as he poured himself some water in the serving area in the corner. He walked back with his water, bringing the pitcher and an extra glass with him. He set them on the table between us. "Sometimes things can get pretty hot in here. We have a lot to do this morning. Please feel free whenever you'd like."

"Thanks," I stammered. I was grateful for the gesture but more unsure than ever what this was all about.

"Tom," said Bud abruptly, "I've asked you to come today for one reason—an important reason."

"Okay," I said evenly, trying to mask the anxiety I was feeling.

"You have a problem—a problem you're going to have to solve if you're going to make it at Zagrum."

I felt as if I'd been kicked in the stomach. I groped for some appropriate word or sound, but my mind was racing and words failed me. I was immediately conscious of the pounding of my heart and the sensation of blood draining from my face.

As successful as I had been in my career, one of my hidden weaknesses was that I was too easily knocked off balance. I had learned to compensate by training the muscles in my face and eyes to relax so that no sudden twitch would betray my alarm. And now, it was as if my face instinctively knew that it had to detach itself from my heart or I would be found out to be the same cowering third-grader who broke into an anxious sweat, hoping for a "well done" sticker, every time Mrs. Lee passed back the homework.

Finally I managed to say, "A problem? What do you mean?"

"Do you really want to know?" asked Bud.

"I'm not sure. I guess I need to, from the sound of it."

"Yes," Bud agreed, "you do."

2 A Problem

"You have a problem," Bud continued. "The people at work know it, your wife knows it, your mother-in-law knows it. I'll bet even your neighbors know it." Despite the digs, he was smiling warmly. "The problem is that *you* don't know it."

I was taken aback. How could I know I had a problem if I didn't even know what the problem was? "I'm afraid I don't know what you mean," I said, trying to exhibit calm.

Bud nodded. "Consider a few experiences," he said. "For example, think of times when you've known that your wife needed the car next and you noticed that it was almost out of fuel. Have you ever taken it home anyway, telling yourself that she could fill it just as easily as you?"

I thought about it for a moment. "I suppose I've done that, yes." *But so what?* I wondered.

"Or have you ever promised to spend time with the kids but backed out at the last minute because something more appealing came up?"

My mind turned to my boy, Todd. It was true that I avoided doing much with him anymore. I didn't think that was entirely my fault, however.

"Or, under similar circumstances," he went on, "have you ever taken the kids where they wanted to go but made them feel guilty about it?"

Yeah, but at least I took them, I said to myself. *Doesn't that count for something?*

"Or how about this one: have you ever parked in a handicapped-only parking zone and then faked a limp so that people wouldn't think you were a jerk?"

"Absolutely not," I said in defense.

"No? Well, have you ever parked where you shouldn't and then sprinted from the car with such purpose that observers would think you just *had* to park there?"

I fidgeted uncomfortably. "Maybe."

"Or have you ever let a coworker do something that you knew would get him into trouble when you easily could have warned or stopped him?"

I didn't say anything.

"And speaking of the workplace," he continued, "have you ever kept some important information to yourself, even when you knew a colleague would really be helped by it?"

I had to admit, I had done that.

"Or are you sometimes disdainful toward the people around you? Do you ever scold them for their laziness or incompetence, for example?"

"I don't know if I *scold* them," I said weakly.

"So what do you do when you think others are incompetent?" Bud asked.

I shrugged. "I guess I try to get them to change in other ways."

"So do you indulge people with kindness and other 'soft stuff' you can think of in order to get them to do what you want? Even though you still feel scornful toward them?"

I didn't think that was fair. "Actually, I think I try pretty hard to treat people right," I countered.

Bud paused for a moment. "I'm sure you do, Tom," he said. "But let me ask you a question. How do you feel when you're 'treating them right,' as you say? Are you still feeling that they're a problem?"

"I'm not sure I know what you mean," I replied.

"What I mean is, do you feel that you have to 'put up' with people—that you have to work pretty hard to succeed as a manager when you're stuck with some of the people you're stuck with?"

"Stuck?" I asked, stalling for time. The truth was, I understood what Bud was saying, but I disagreed with what I thought he was implying. I was trying frantically to find an acceptable way to defend myself. "I suppose it's true that I think some people are lazy and incompetent," I finally replied. "Are you saying I'm wrong about that—that *no one* is lazy and incompetent?" My inflection on "no one" was too strong, and I cursed myself for letting my frustration show.

Bud shook his head. "Not at all. Some people are lazy. And I, for one, am incompetent at a whole bunch of things." He paused for a moment. "So what do you do when you're confronted with someone you believe is lazy or incompetent?"

I thought about it. "That depends. I'm pretty direct with some people, but with others that doesn't work very well so I try to get them going in other ways. Some I try to encourage, and others I feel like I have to outsmart or outmaneuver. But I've learned to keep my smile most of the time, and that seems to help. I think I do a pretty good job with people, actually."

Bud nodded. "I understand. But when we're finished, I think you may feel differently."

The comment unsettled me. "What's wrong with treating people well?" I protested.

"Nothing. If that's what one is actually doing," Bud said. "But I think you might discover that you aren't treating people as well as you think. You may be doing more damage than you know."

"Damage?" I repeated. A rush of worry flushed my cheeks. Attempting to keep my emotions under control, I said, "I'm afraid you're going to have to explain that to me." The words sounded too combative, even to my own ear, and my cheeks flushed all the more.

"I'll be happy to," he said calmly. "I can help you learn what your problem is—and what to do about it. That's why we're meeting." He paused, and then added, "I can help you because I have the same problem."

3   *Self-Deception*

"Do you have kids, Tom?"

I was grateful for the simple question and felt the life come back to my face. "Why, yes, one actually. His name is Todd. He's 16."

Bud smiled. "Do you remember how you felt when Todd was born—how it seemed to change your perspective on life?"

I strained to find my way back to the memories of Todd's birth—through the pain, through the heartache. Diagnosed at a fairly young age with attention deficit disorder, he had been a difficult child, and my wife, Laura, and I clashed constantly over what to do with him. Things had only gotten worse as he grew older. Todd and I didn't have much of a relationship. But at Bud's invitation, I attempted a remembrance of the time and emotion surrounding his birth. "Yes, I remember," I began pensively. "I remember holding him close, pondering my hope for his life—feeling inadequate, even overwhelmed, but at the same time grateful." The memory lessened for a moment the pain I felt in the present.

"That was the way it was for me too," Bud said. "Would you mind if I told you a story that began with the birth of my first child, David?"

"Please," I said, happy to hear his story rather than relive my own.

"I was a young lawyer at the time," he began, "working long hours at one of the most prestigious firms in the country. One of the deals I worked on was a major financing project that involved about 30 banks worldwide. Our client was the lead lender on the deal.

"It was a complicated project involving many lawyers. I was the second most junior member of the team and had chief responsibility for the drafting of 50 or so agreements that sat underneath the major lending contract. It was a big, sexy deal involving international travel, numbers with lots of zeros, and high-profile characters.

"A week after I'd been assigned to the project, Nancy and I found out she was pregnant. It was a marvelous time for us. David was born eight months later, on December 16. Before the birth, I worked hard to wrap up or assign my projects so that I could take three weeks off with our new baby. I don't think I've ever been happier in my life.

"But then came a phone call. It was December 29. The lead partner on the deal was calling me. I was needed at an 'all hands' meeting in San Francisco.

"'How long?' I asked.

"'Until the deal closes—could be three weeks, could be three months. We're here until it's done,' he said.

"I was crushed. The thought of leaving Nancy and David alone in our Alexandria, Virginia, home left me desperately sad. It took me two days to wrap up my affairs in DC before I reluctantly boarded a plane for San Francisco. I left my young family at the curb at Reagan National Airport. With a photo album under my arm, I tore myself away from them and turned through the doors of the terminal.

"By the time I arrived at our San Francisco offices, I was the last one in on the deal. Even the guy from our London office beat me. I settled into the last remaining guest office, which was on the 21st floor. The deal headquarters, and everyone else, was on floor 25.

"I hunkered down and got to work. Most of the action was on 25—meetings, negotiations among all the parties, everything. But I was alone on 21—alone with my work and my photo album, which sat open on my desk.

"I worked from 6 AM till after midnight every day. Three times a day I would go down to the deli in the lobby and purchase a bagel, a sandwich, or a salad. Then I'd go back up to 21 and eat while poring over the documents.

"If you had asked me at the time what my objective was, I would have told you that I was 'drafting the best possible documents to protect our client and close the deal,' or something to that effect. But you should know a couple of other things about my experience in San Francisco.

"All of the negotiations that were central to the documents I was working on were happening on the 25th floor. These 25th-floor negotiations should have been very important to me because every change to the deal had to be accounted for in all the documents I was drafting. But I didn't go up to 25 much.

"In fact, after 10 days of lobby deli food, I found out that food was being served around the clock in the main conference room on 25 for everyone working on the deal. I was upset that no one had told me about it. And twice during those 10 days I was chewed out for failing to incorporate some of the latest changes into my documents. No one had told me about those either! Another time I was reprimanded for being hard to find. And on two occasions during that period, the lead partner asked for my opinion on issues that had never occurred to me—issues that would have occurred to me had I been thinking. They were in my area of responsibility. He shouldn't have had to do my job for me.

"Now, let me ask you a question, Tom. Just from the little bit you now know about my San Francisco experience, would you say that I was really committed to 'drafting the best possible documents to protect our client and close the deal'?"

"No," I said, shaking my head, surprised at the ease with which I was about to harpoon Bud Jefferson. "It sounds like you were preoccupied with something else. It doesn't seem like you were engaged in the project at all."

"That's right," he agreed. "I *wasn't* engaged in it. And do you think the lead partner could tell?"

"I think that after those 10 days it would have been obvious," I offered.

"He could tell well enough to chew me out a couple of times at the very least," Bud said. "How about this: Do you suppose he would say that I'd bought into the vision? Or that I was committed? Or that I was being maximally helpful to others on the deal?"

"No, I don't think so. By keeping yourself isolated, you were putting things at risk—*his* things," I answered.

"I have to agree with you," Bud said. "I had become a problem, no question about it. I wasn't engaged in the deal, wasn't committed, hadn't caught the vision, was making trouble for others, and so on. But consider this: How do you suppose I would have responded had someone accused me of not being committed or not being engaged? Do you think I would have agreed with them?"

I pondered the question. "I doubt it. It's kind of tough to agree with people when they're criticizing you. You probably would have felt defensive if someone had accused you like that."

"And consider the defenses I could have levied," Bud said, nodding in agreement. "Think about it: Who left behind a new baby to go to San Francisco? I did. And who was working 20-hour days? I was." He was becoming more animated. "And who was forced to work alone four floors below the others? I was. And to whom did people even forget to mention basic details like food plans? To me. So from my perspective, who was making things difficult for whom?"

"Hmm, I guess you would have seen *others* as being the main cause of the trouble," I answered, finding the irony interesting.

"You'd better believe it," he said. "And how about being committed, engaged, and catching the vision? Do you see that from my perspective, not only was I committed, but I just might've been the most committed person on the deal? Because from my point of view, no one had as many challenges to deal with as I had. And I was working hard in spite of them."

"That's right," I said, relaxing back into my chair and nodding affirmatively. "You *would* have felt that way."

"So let's think about it again." Bud rose again and began pacing. "Remember the problem. I was uncommitted, was disengaged, hadn't caught the vision, and was making things more difficult for others on the deal. That's all true. And that's a problem—a big problem. But there was a bigger problem— and it's this problem that you and I need to talk about."

He had my full attention.

"The bigger problem was that I couldn't *see* that I had a problem."

Bud paused for a moment, and then, leaning toward me, he said in a lower, even more earnest tone, "There is no solution to the problem of lack of commitment, for example, without a solution to the bigger problem—the problem that I can't *see* that I'm not committed."

I suddenly started to be uneasy and could feel my face again sag to expressionlessness. I had been caught up in Bud's story and had forgotten that he was telling it to me for a reason. This story was for me. He must have been thinking that *I* had a bigger problem. Despite my efforts to stay coolly detached, my face and ears began to heat up.

"Tom, there's a technical name for the insistent blindness I exhibited in San Francisco. Philosophers and psychologists call it 'self-deception.' At Zagrum, we have a less technical name for it—we call it 'being in the box.' In our way of talking, when we're self-deceived, we're 'in the box.' You're going to learn a lot more about the box, but as a starting point, think of it this way: In one sense, I was 'stuck' in my experience in San Francisco. I was stuck because I had a problem I didn't think I had—a problem I couldn't see. I could see only from my own closed perspective, and I was deeply resistant to any suggestion that the truth was other than what I was thinking. So I was in a box—cut off, closed up, blind. Does that make sense?"

I nodded.

"There's nothing more common in organizations than self-deception," he continued. "For example, think about a person from your work experience who's a big problem—say, someone who's been a major impediment to teamwork."

That was easy—Chuck Staehli, COO of my former employer. He was a jerk, plain and simple. He thought of no one but himself. "Yeah, I know a guy like that."

"Well, here's the question: Does the person you're thinking of believe he's a problem like you believe he is?"

I shook my head vigorously. "No. Definitely not."

"That's usually the case. Identify someone with a problem, and you'll be identifying someone who resists the suggestion that he has one. That's self-deception—the problem of not knowing and resisting the possibility that one has a problem.

"Of all the problems in organizations," Bud said, "self-deception is the most common and the most damaging." He paused to let the point sink in. "Think about it, Tom. You can't make headway solving problems if the people causing those problems refuse to consider how they might be responsible. So at Zagrum, our top strategic initiative is to minimize individual and organizational self-deception."

Bud stood and began to pace. "To underscore why it's so important to us," he said, "I need to tell you about an analogous problem in medicine."

4 The Problem beneath Other Problems

"Have you ever heard of Ignaz Semmelweis?" Bud asked. (He pronounced it "Ignawts Semelvice.")

"No, I don't think so. Is it a sickness or something?"

"No, no," he said with a chuckle. "But close. Semmelweis was a European doctor, an obstetrician, in the mid-1800s. He worked at the Vienna General Hospital, an important research hospital, where he tried to get to the bottom of a horrendous mortality rate among women in the maternity ward. In the section of the ward where Semmelweis practiced, the mortality rate was 1 in 10. Think of it. One in every 10 women giving birth there died! Can you imagine?"

"I wouldn't have let my wife near the place," I said.

"You wouldn't have been alone. Vienna General had such a frightening reputation that some women actually gave birth on the street and *then* went to the hospital."

"I don't blame them," I said.

"The collection of symptoms associated with these deaths," Bud continued, "became known as 'childbed fever.' Conventional medical science at the time called for separate treatment for each symptom. Inflammation meant that excess blood was causing swelling—so they bled the patient or applied leeches. They treated fever the same way. Trouble breathing meant the air was bad—so they improved ventilation. And so on. But nothing worked. More than half of the women who contracted the disease died within days.

"The terrible risk was well known. Semmelweis reported that patients were frequently seen 'kneeling and wringing their hands,' begging to be moved to a second section of the maternity ward, where the mortality rate was 1 in 50—still horrific, but far better than the 1-in-10 rate in Semmelweis's section.

"Semmelweis gradually became obsessed with the problem—in particular with discovering why the mortality rate in one section of the maternity ward was so much higher than the rate in the other. The only obvious difference between the sections was that Semmelweis's section— the section that performed the worst—was attended by doctors, while the other section was attended by midwives. He couldn't see why that would explain the difference, so he tried to equalize every other factor among the maternity patients. He standardized everything from birthing positions to ventilation and diet. He even standardized the way the laundry was done. He looked at every possibility but could find no answer. Nothing he tried made any measurable difference in the mortality rates.

"But then something happened. He took a four-month leave to visit another hospital, and upon his return he discovered that the death rate had fallen significantly in his section of the ward in his absence."

"Really?"

"Yes. He didn't know why, but it had definitely fallen. He dug in to find the reason. Gradually, his inquiry led him to think about the possible significance of research done by the doctors on cadavers."

"Cadavers?"

"Yes. Remember, Vienna General was a teaching and research hospital. Many of the doctors split their time between research on cadavers and treatment of live patients.

They hadn't seen any problem with that practice because there was as yet no understanding of germs. All they knew were symptoms. And in examining his own work practices compared with the practices of those who had worked for him in his absence, Semmelweis discovered that the only significant difference was that he, Semmelweis, spent far more time doing research on the cadavers.

"From these observations, he developed a theory of childbed fever, a theory that became the precursor to germ theory. He concluded that 'particles' from cadavers and other diseased patients were being transmitted to healthy patients *on the hands of the physicians*. So he immediately instituted a policy requiring physicians to wash their hands thoroughly in a chlorine-and-lime solution before examining any patient. And you know what happened?"

I shook my head. "What?"

"The death rate immediately fell to 1 in 100."

"So he was right," I said, almost under my breath. "The doctors were the carriers."

"Yes. In fact, Semmelweis once sadly remarked, 'Only God knows the number of patients who went prematurely to their graves because of me.' Imagine living with *that*. The doctors were doing the best they knew how, but they were carrying a disease they knew nothing about. It caused a multitude of debilitating symptoms, all of which could be prevented by a single act once the common cause of the symptoms was discovered—what was later identified as a germ."

Bud stopped. He put his hands on the table and leaned toward me. "There is a similar germ that is spread in organizations—a germ we all carry to one extent or another, a germ that kills leadership effectiveness and teamwork, a germ that causes a multitude of 'people problems,' a germ that can be isolated and neutralized."

"What is it?" I asked.

"Just what we've been talking about," Bud replied. "Self-deception — 'the box.' Or, more precisely, self-deception is the disease. What we're going to learn about is the germ that causes it. And what I'm suggesting, Tom, is that, like the discovery of the cause of childbed fever, the discovery of the cause of self-deception amounts to the revelation of a sort of unifying theory, an explanation that shows how the apparently disparate collection of symptoms we call 'people problems' — from problems in leadership to problems in motivation and everything in between — are all caused by the same thing. With this knowledge, people problems can be solved with an efficiency that has never been possible before. There is a clear way to attack and solve them — not one by one but in one disciplined stroke."

"That's a bold claim," I said.

"Indeed," Bud responded. "But I don't intend for you to take my word for it. I'm going to attempt to help you discover it for yourself. We need you to understand it because you need to make sure the strategies that follow from it are implemented in your division."

"Okay," I said.

"To begin with," he said, "I think you might be interested to know how I failed at this when I first joined Zagrum."

5 Beneath Effective Leadership

"After nine years at the law firm," Bud began, "I left to become general counsel of Sierra Product Systems. Do you remember Sierra?"

Sierra had pioneered several of the processes that Zagrum had exploited to climb to its place at the top of the high-tech manufacturing heap. "Of course," I replied. "Their technologies changed the industry. Whatever happened to them?"

"They were acquired—by Zagrum Company."

"Really? I never heard that."

"The deal was sort of complicated. But the long and short of it is that Zagrum acquired most of Sierra's useful intellectual property—patents and so on. That was 16 years ago. At the time, I was COO of Sierra and came to Zagrum as part of the deal. I had no idea what I was getting into." Bud reached for his glass and took a drink. "At the time, Zagrum was a bit of a mystery. But I was introduced to the mystery of Zagrum in a hurry—in my second major meeting, to be exact.

"Being intimately familiar with the key acquisitions from Sierra, I joined Zagrum as part of the executive team. In my first meeting, I was given several difficult assignments to complete before the next meeting in two weeks. It was a heavy load, learning the business and all.

"At last, on the night before the next meeting, there was only one assignment that I'd yet to complete. It was late, and I was tired. Given all I'd accomplished and been through to do it, this one remaining assignment seemed inconsequential. So I let it go.

"At the meeting the next day, I reported my achievements, made recommendations, and shared the important information I had gathered. Then I told the group that because all my time had been taken up with these other assignments, not to mention all the obstacles I'd encountered, there was one assignment I hadn't yet completed.

"I'll never forget what happened next. Lou Herbert, who was then president of the company, turned to Kate Stenarude, who at the time occupied the position I have now, and asked *her* to take that assignment for the next meeting. The meeting then continued with others' reports. Nothing more was made of it, but I noticed that I was the only person in the group who had left something undone.

"I spent the rest of the meeting lost in my own thoughts—feeling embarrassed, feeling small, wondering if I belonged, wondering if I *wanted* to belong.

"The meeting closed, and I packed my documents into my briefcase as others chatted. I didn't feel part of the group at that moment and was quietly slipping past some of my bantering colleagues toward the door when I felt a hand on my shoulder.

"I turned and saw Lou smiling, gazing at me with his gentle yet penetrating eyes. He asked if I'd mind if he walked with me back to my office. To my surprise after what he had just done to me in the meeting, I replied that I would welcome it."

Bud paused for a moment, pulling himself from the memory. "You don't know Lou, Tom, and probably haven't been here long enough to know the stories, but Lou Herbert is a legend. He was personally responsible for taking a mediocre, inconsequential company and making it into a juggernaut—sometimes in spite of, and sometimes even because of, his weaknesses. Everyone who worked at Zagrum during his era was fiercely loyal to him."

"I've heard a few stories, actually," I said. "And I remember from my work at Tetrix how even the top folks there seemed to admire him—Joe Alvarez in particular, the Tetrix CEO, who considered Lou the pioneer of the industry."

"He's right," Bud agreed. "Lou *was* the industry pioneer. But Joe doesn't know the extent of his pioneering. That's what *you're* going to learn," he emphasized. "Lou's been retired for years now, but he still comes around a few times a month to see how we're doing. His insight is invaluable. We still keep an office for him.

"Anyway, I knew much of his legend before I joined the company. So perhaps you can understand my warring emotions after the meeting I just described. I felt that I'd been slighted, but I was also supremely worried about Lou's opinion of me. And then he asked if he could walk me to my office! I was glad to have him walk with me but also afraid—of what, though, I didn't know.

"He asked me how my move had been, whether my family was settled and happy, and how I was enjoying the challenges at Zagrum. He was saddened to hear that Nancy was having a hard time with the move and promised to call her personally to see if there was anything he could do—a call he placed that very night.

"When we arrived at my office, before I could turn to go in, he took me by both shoulders with his strong, lean hands. He looked straight into my eyes, a look of gentle concern written in the lines across his weathered face. 'Bud,' he said, 'we're happy to have you with us. You're a talented man and a good man. You add a lot to the team. But you won't ever let us down again, will you?'"

"Are you kidding me?" I asked incredulously. "He said *that*?"

"Yes."

"Nothing against Lou," I said, "but I think that was a little uncalled for, given all you'd done. You can scare away a lot of people saying things like that."

"That's true," Bud agreed. "But you know something? It didn't happen that way for me. With Lou, in that moment, I wasn't offended. And in a way, I was even inspired. I found myself saying, 'No, Lou. I won't. I won't ever let you down again.'

"Now I know that sounds corny. But that's the way it was with Lou. He very rarely did things by the book. If 100 people had tried to do what Lou did to me in that meeting and afterward, only 1 in 100 could have invited my cooperation, as Lou did, rather than my resentment. By the book, it shouldn't have worked. But it worked anyway. And with Lou, it usually did. The question, Tom, is *why—why* did it work?"

That was a good question. "I don't know," I finally said, shrugging my shoulders. Then, almost as an afterthought, I said, "Maybe you just knew that Lou cared about you, so you didn't feel as threatened as you might have otherwise."

Bud smiled and sat down again in the seat across from me. "So you think I could *tell* that—how Lou was feeling about me."

"Yeah, I think you probably could."

"And so you're saying, then, Tom, that I was primarily responding to how Lou was regarding me—at least to how I thought he was regarding me—and that his regard, to me, was more important than merely his words or his actions. Is that what you're suggesting?"

·I pondered the question for a moment, thinking about the things I cared about in my interactions with others. I *did* pay attention to how I thought others were seeing me—what my wife, Laura, was thinking about me, for example, or whether I thought she was just thinking of herself. My responses to her and to others always seemed to be informed by what I thought they were thinking of me. "Yes, I guess I *am* suggesting that," I agreed. "If I feel like someone is just thinking of himself, I usually discount everything he says."

Bud nodded. "We had a good example of that here a couple of years ago. Two people over in Building 6 were having a hard time working together. One of them, Gabe, came to me to talk about it and said, 'I don't know what to do here. I can't get Leon to respond and cooperate with me. It doesn't matter what I do; Leon doesn't seem to think that I have any interest in him. I go out of my way to ask about his family. I invite him to lunch. I've done everything I can think of doing, but nothing helps.'

" 'I want you to consider something, Gabe,' I said to him. 'Really think about it. When you're going out of your way to do all those things for Leon so that he'll know you have an interest in him, what are you most interested in—*him* or his opinion of *you?*'

"I think Gabe was a little surprised by the question. 'Perhaps Leon thinks you're not really interested in him,' I continued, 'because you're really more interested in yourself.'

"Gabe finally understood the problem, but it was a painful moment. It was up to him, then, to figure out what to do about it, applying some of the things that you and I are going to cover today—ideas, by the way, that apply as much to our relationships at home as they do to our relationships at work. Let me give you an example of that, closer to home."

Bud smiled at me. "You've probably never had an argument with your wife, now, have you?"

I burst out in a too-eager laugh. "Just a couple."

"Well, my wife, Nancy, and I were in the middle of one of those a number of years back. It was the morning, before work. As I recall, she was upset that I hadn't cleaned the dishes the night before, and I was upset that she was so upset about it. Do you get the picture?"

"Oh yeah, I've been there," I said, thinking of the argument I'd had with Laura that very morning.

"After a while, Nancy and I had actually worked our ways to opposite sides of the room," Bud continued. "I was tiring of our little 'discussion,' which was making me late for work, and decided to apologize and put an end to it. I walked over to her and said, 'I'm sorry, Nancy,' and bent down to kiss her.

"Our lips met, if at all, only for a millisecond. It was the world's shortest kiss. I didn't intend it that way, but it was all either of us could muster.

" 'You don't mean it,' she said quietly, as I backed slowly away. And she was right, of course—for just the reason we've been talking about. The way I really felt came through. I felt wronged, burdened, and unappreciated, and I couldn't cover it up—even with a kiss. But I remember wandering down the hall toward the garage, shaking my head and muttering to myself. Now I had more evidence of my wife's unreasonableness—she couldn't even accept an apology!

"But here's the point, Tom: Was there an apology to accept?"

"No, because you didn't really mean it, just like Nancy said."

"That's right. My words said, 'I'm sorry,' but my feelings didn't, and it was the way I was feeling—revealed as it was through my voice, my gaze, my posture, my level of interest in her needs, and so on—it was *that* that she was responding to."

Bud paused, and I thought of that morning with Laura: her face, a face that once radiated energy, concern, and love for life, now obscured by resignation to a deep hurt, her words tearing holes in whatever convictions I still held for our marriage. "I don't feel like I know you anymore, Tom," she had said. "And what's worse, I get the feeling most of the time that you don't really care to know *me*. It's like I weigh you down or something. I don't know the last time I felt love from you. It's all coldness now. You just bury yourself in your work— even when you're home. And to be honest, I don't really have strong feelings for you, either. I wish I did, but everything is just kind of blah. Our life together isn't really together at all. We just live our lives separately while living in the same house, passing each other every now and then, inquiring about calendars and common events. We even manage to smile, but it's all lies. There's no feeling behind it."

"As you suggested, Tom," I heard Bud say, calling me back from my troubles, "we often can sense how others are feeling toward us, can't we? Given a little time, we can tell when we're being coped with, manipulated, or outsmarted. We can detect the hypocrisy. We can feel the blame concealed beneath veneers of niceness. And we typically resent it. In the workplace, for example, it won't matter if the other person tries managing by walking around, sitting on the edge of the chair to practice active listening, inquiring about family members in order to show interest, or using any other skill they may have learned in order to be more effective. What we'll know and respond to is how that person is *regarding* us when doing those things."

My thoughts turned to Chuck Staehli again. "Yeah, I know what you're talking about," I said. "Do you know Chuck Staehli, the COO over at Tetrix?"

"About six-foot-four, thinning reddish hair, narrow intense eyes?" asked Bud.

"That's him. Well, it took me about two minutes with him to know that he felt the world revolved around him—and if not the world, then certainly everyone in his organization. I remember, for example, being on a conference call with Joe Alvarez after a hectic October spent fixing a bug in one of our products. It was a Herculean effort that consumed nearly all of my time and 80 percent of the time of one of my groups. On the call, Joe offered congratulations for a job well done. Guess who accepted all the praise?"

"Staehli?"

"Yes, Staehli. He barely acknowledged us—and it was in such an undervalued way that it was worse than if he hadn't. He just lapped it all up and basked in the glory. I think in that moment he really thought he *was* responsible. It made me sick, quite frankly. And that's just one of many examples."

Bud was listening with interest, and suddenly I became aware of what I was doing—criticizing my old boss in front of my new one. I felt that I should shut up. Immediately. "Anyway, it just seemed that Chuck was a good example of what you're talking about." I leaned back in my chair to signal that I was done, hoping that I hadn't said too much.

If Bud was alarmed by anything, he didn't show it. "Yeah, that's a good example," he said. "Now compare Staehli with Lou. Or, more precisely, compare the *influence* that each of them had on others. Would you say, for example, that Staehli inspired in you the same kind of effort, the same level of results, as Lou inspired in me?"

That was easy. "No way," I said. "Staehli didn't inspire hard work or devotion at all. Don't get me wrong. I worked hard anyway because I had a career of my own to worry about. But no one ever went out of their way to help him."

"Notice that some people—like Lou, for example—inspire devotion and commitment in others, even when they're interpersonally clumsy," said Bud. "The fact that they haven't attended many seminars or that they've never learned the latest techniques hardly matters. They seem to produce anyway. And they inspire those around them to do the same. Some of the best leaders in our company fall in this category. They don't always say or do the 'right' things, but people love working with them. They get results.

"But then there are other people—like Chuck Staehli, as you described him—who have a very different influence. Even if they do all the 'right' things interpersonally—even if they apply all the latest skills and techniques to their communications and tasks—it won't matter. People ultimately resent them and their tactics. And so they end up failing as leaders—failing because they provoke people to resist them."

Everything Bud was saying seemed true when applied to Chuck Staehli, but I wondered whether he was going too far. "I get what you're saying," I said, "I think I even agree with it. But are you suggesting that people skills don't matter at all? I'm not sure *that's* right."

"No. I certainly don't mean to suggest that. But I *am* suggesting that people skills are never *primary*. In my experience, they can be valuable when used by people like Lou—they can reduce misunderstandings and clumsiness. But they're not so helpful when used by people like Staehli, as you described him, for they just create resentment in the people one is trying to 'skill' or 'smooth' into doing something. Whether or not people skills are effective depends on something deeper."

"Deeper?"

"Yes, deeper than behavior and skill. That's what Lou— and my reaction to him—taught me the day of that second meeting here at Zagrum. *And* what he taught me at the beginning of the very next day when he and I met for a day-long meeting."

"You mean—?"

"Yes, Tom," Bud answered, before I had voiced the question. "Lou did for me what I'm now beginning to do for you. They used to be called 'Lou Meetings,'" he added with a grin and a knowing look.

"Remember, I have the same problem that you have."

6 *The Deep Choice That Determines Influence*

"So what's this something deeper?" I asked curiously.

"What I've already introduced to you—self-deception," Bud replied. "Whether I'm *in* or *out of* the box."

"Okay," I said slowly, wanting to know more.

"As we've been talking about, no matter what we're doing on the outside, people respond primarily to how we're feeling about them on the inside. And how we're feeling about them depends on whether we're in or out of the box concerning them. Let me illustrate that point further with a couple of examples.

"About a year ago, I flew from Dallas to Phoenix on a flight that had open seating. While boarding, I overheard the boarding agent say that the plane was not sold out but that there would be very few unused seats. I felt lucky and relieved to find a window seat open with a vacant seat beside it about a third of the way back on the plane. Passengers still in need of seats continued streaming down the aisle, their eyes scanning and evaluating the desirability of their dwindling seating options. I set my briefcase on the vacant middle seat, took out that day's paper, and started to read. I remember peering over the top corner of the paper at the people who were coming down the aisle. At the sight of body language that said my briefcase's seat was being considered, I spread the paper wider, making the seat look as undesirable as possible. Do you get the picture?"

"Oh yeah."

"Good. Now let me ask you a question: On the surface, what *behaviors* was I engaged in on the plane—what were some of the things I was *doing?*"

"Well, you were being kind of a jerk, for one thing," I answered.

"Now that's certainly true," Bud agreed, breaking into a broad smile, "but that's not quite what I mean—not yet, anyway. I mean, what specific actions was I taking on the plane? What were my actions or behaviors?"

I pictured the situation. "You were . . . taking two seats. Is that the kind of thing you mean?"

"Sure. What else?"

"Uh . . . you were reading the paper. You were watching for people who might want to sit in the seat next to you. To be very basic, you were sitting."

"Okay, good enough," said Bud. "Here's another question: While I was doing those behaviors, how was I seeing the people who were looking for seats? What were they to me?"

"I'd say that you saw them as threats, maybe nuisances or problems—something like that."

Bud nodded. "Would you say that I considered the needs of those still looking for seats to be as legitimate as my own?"

"Not at all. Your needs counted, and everyone else's were secondary—if that," I answered, surprised by my bluntness. "You were kind of seeing yourself as the kingpin."

Bud laughed, obviously enjoying the comment. "Well said, well said." Then he continued, more seriously, "You're right. On that plane, if others counted at all, their needs and desires counted far less than mine. Now compare that experience with this one: About six months ago, Nancy and I took a trip to Florida. Somehow there was a mistake in the ticketing process, and we weren't seated together. The flight was mostly full, and the flight attendant was having a difficult time trying to find a way to seat us together. As we stood in the aisle trying to figure out a solution, a woman holding a hastily folded newspaper came up behind us, from the rear of the plane, and said, 'Excuse me—if you need two seats together, I believe the seat next to me is vacant. I'd be happy to sit in one of your seats.'

"Now think of this woman. How would you say that she saw us—did she see us as threats, nuisances, or problems?"

"No," I said, shaking my head. "It seems like she just saw you as people in need of seats who would like to sit together. That's probably more basic than what you're looking for, but—"

"On the contrary," Bud said, "that's a terrific way to put it. She just saw us as people—we're going to come back to that in a moment. Now let's compare the way this woman apparently saw others with the way I saw those who were loading onto the plane in my story involving the briefcase. You said that I saw myself as kind of the kingpin—more important than others, with needs that were greater."

I nodded.

"Is that the way this woman seemed to see herself and others?" he asked. "Did she, like me, seem to privilege her own needs and desires over the needs and desires of others?"

"It doesn't seem like it, no," I answered. "It's sort of like from her point of view, under the circumstances, your needs and her needs counted about the same."

"That's how it felt," Bud said, nodding. He got up and walked toward the far end of the conference table. "Here we have two situations in which a person was seated on a plane next to an empty seat, evidently reading the paper and observing others who were still in need of seats on the plane. That's what was happening on the surface—behaviorally."

He opened two large mahogany doors in the wall at the far end of the table, revealing a large whiteboard. "But notice how different this similar experience was for me and for this woman. I minimized others; she didn't. I felt anxious, uptight, irritated, threatened, and angry, while she appeared to have had no such negative emotions at all. I sat there blaming others who might be interested in my briefcase's seat—maybe one looked too happy, another too grim, another had too many carry-ons, another looked too talkative, and so on. She, on the other hand, seemed not to have blamed but to have understood—whether happy, grim, loaded with carry-ons, talkative, or not—they needed to sit *somewhere*. And if so, why shouldn't the seat next to her—and in her case, even her *own* seat—be as rightly theirs as any others?

"Now here's a question for you," Bud continued. "Isn't it the case that the people getting on both planes were people with comparable hopes, needs, cares, and fears, and that all of them had more or less the same need to sit?"

That seemed about right. "Yes. I'd agree with that."

"If that's true, then I had a big problem—because I wasn't seeing the people on the plane like that at all. My view was that I somehow was entitled or superior to those who were still looking for seats. Which is to say that I wasn't really seeing them as people at all. They were more like objects to me in that moment than people."

"Yeah, I can see that," I agreed.

"Notice how my view of both myself and others was distorted from what we agreed was the reality," Bud said. "Although the truth was that all of us were people with more or less the same need to sit, I wasn't seeing the situation that way. So my view of the world was a systematically incorrect way of seeing others and myself. I saw others as less than they were—as objects with needs and desires somehow secondary to and less legitimate than mine. But I couldn't see the problem with what I was doing. I was self-deceived—or, in the box. The lady who offered us her seat, on the other hand, saw others and the situation clearly, without bias. She saw others as they were, as people like herself, with similar needs and desires. She saw straightforwardly. She was out of the box.

"So the inner experiences of two people," he went on, "although they exhibited the same external behaviors, were entirely different. This difference is important enough that I want to emphasize it with a diagram." At this, he turned to the board and spent a minute drawing the following:

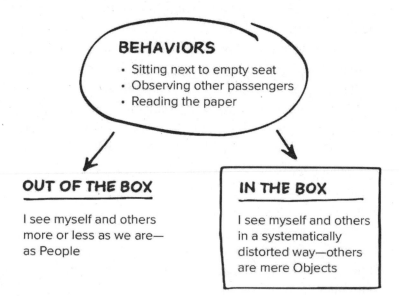

BEHAVIORS
- Sitting next to empty seat
- Observing other passengers
- Reading the paper

OUT OF THE BOX

I see myself and others more or less as we are— as People

IN THE BOX

I see myself and others in a systematically distorted way—others are mere Objects

"It's like this, Tom," Bud said, stepping to the side of the board so that I could see. "Whatever I might be 'doing' on the surface—whether it be, for example, sitting, observing others, reading the paper, whatever—I'm being one of two fundamental ways when I'm doing it. Either I'm seeing others straightforwardly as they are—as people like me who have needs and desires as legitimate as my own—or I'm not. As I heard Kate put it once: One way, I experience myself as *a* person among people. The other way, I experience myself as *the* person among objects. One way, I'm out of the box; the other way, I'm in the box. Does that make sense?"

I was thinking about a situation that had occurred a week earlier. Someone in my department had made herself into a terrible nuisance, and I couldn't see how this in-the-box and out-of-the-box distinction applied. In fact, if anything, the situation seemed to undercut what Bud was talking about. "I'm not sure," I said. "Let me give you a situation and you tell me how it fits."

"Fair enough," he said, taking his seat.

"I have a conference room around the corner from my office where I often go to think and strategize. The people in my department know that the room is like a second office to me and are careful now, after a few altercations over the last month, not to schedule it without my knowing. Last week, however, someone in the department went in and used it. Not only did she use the room without scheduling it, but she erased all my notes from the whiteboard. What do you think of that?"

"Under the circumstances, I'd say that was pretty poor judgment on her part."

Nodding, I said, "I was peeved, to say the least. It took me a while to reconstruct what I had done, and I'm still not sure that I have everything right."

I was about to tell more—about how I immediately had her called into my office, refused a handshake, and then told her without even asking her to sit down that she was never to do that again or she would be looking for a new job. But then I thought better of it. "How does self-deception fit into *that* scenario?" I asked.

"Let me ask you a few questions," Bud answered, "and then maybe you can tell me. What kinds of thoughts and feelings did you have about this woman when you found out what she'd done?"

"Well . . . I guess I thought she wasn't very careful."

Bud nodded with an inquisitive look that invited me to say more.

"And I suppose I thought it was stupid of her to do what she did without asking anybody." I paused and then added, "It was pretty presumptuous of her, don't you think?"

"Certainly not very wise," Bud agreed. "Anything more?"

"No, that's about what I remember."

"Let me ask you this, then: Do you know what she wanted to use the room for?"

"Well, no. But why should that matter? It doesn't change the fact that she shouldn't have been using it, does it?"

"Perhaps not," Bud answered. "But let me ask you another question: Do you know her name?"

The question caught me by surprise. I thought for a moment. I wasn't sure I'd ever heard her name. Had my secretary mentioned it? Or did she say it herself when she extended her hand to greet me? I searched my memory, but there was nothing.

But why should that matter, anyway? I thought to myself, emboldened. *So I don't know her name. So what? Does that make me wrong or something?* "No, I guess I don't know it, or I can't remember," I said.

Bud nodded. "Now here's the question I'd really like you to consider. Assuming that this woman is, in fact, careless, stupid, and presumptuous, do you suppose that she's *as* careless, stupid, and presumptuous as you accused her of being when all this happened?"

"Well, I didn't really accuse her."

"Not in your words, perhaps, but have you had any interaction with her since the incident?"

I thought of the ice-cold reception I gave her and the offer of her hand rebuffed.

"Yeah, just once," I said meekly.

Bud must have noticed the change in my voice, for he dropped his voice slightly and lost his matter-of-fact tone. "Tom, I want you to imagine that you were her when you met. What do you think she felt from you?"

The answer, of course, was obvious. She couldn't have felt worse if I'd hit her with a two-by-four. I remembered the tremor in her voice and her uncertain yet hurried steps as she left my office. I wondered now for the first time how I must have hurt her and what she must be feeling. I imagined that she must now be quite insecure and worried, especially since everyone in the department seemed to know about what had happened. "Yeah," I said slowly, "looking back on it, I'm afraid I didn't handle the situation very well."

"Then let me come back to my prior question," Bud said. "Do you suppose that your view of this woman at the time made her seem worse than she really was?"

I paused before answering, not because I wasn't sure, but because I wanted to collect my composure. "Well, maybe.

But that doesn't change the fact that she did something she shouldn't have, does it?" I added.

"Not at all. And we'll get to that. But right now, the question I want you to consider is this: Whatever she was doing—be it right or wrong—was your view of her more like *my* view of the people on the plane or more like the view of the woman I told you about?"

I thought about that for a moment.

"Think of it this way," Bud added, pointing at the diagram on the board. "Were you regarding her as a person like your-self, with similar hopes and needs, or was she just an object to you—as you said, just a threat, a nuisance, or a problem?"

"I guess she might've been just an object to me," I said finally.

"So now, how would you say this self-deception stuff applies? Would you say you were *in* or *out of* the box?"

"I guess I was probably *in* it," I said.

"That's worth thinking about, Tom. Because this distinc-tion," he said, pointing again at the diagram, "reveals what was beneath Lou's success—and Zagrum's, for that matter. Because Lou was usually out of the box, he saw straight-forwardly. He saw people as they were—as people. And he found a way to build a company of people who see that way much more than people in most organizations do. If you want to know the secret of Zagrum's success, it's that we've devel-oped a culture where people are simply invited to see others as people. And being seen and treated straightforwardly, peo-ple respond accordingly. That's what I felt—and returned—to Lou."

That sounded great, but it seemed too simplistic to be the element that set Zagrum apart. "It can't really be that simple, can it, Bud? I mean, if Zagrum's secret were that basic, everyone would have duplicated it by now."

"Don't misunderstand," said Bud. "I'm not minimizing the importance of, for example, getting smart and skilled people into the company or working hard or any other number of things that are important to Zagrum's success. But notice—everyone else has duplicated all of *that* stuff, but they've yet to duplicate our results. And that's because they don't know how much smarter smart people are, how much more skilled skilled people get, and how much harder hardworking people work when they see, and are seen, straightforwardly—as people.

"And don't forget," he continued, "self-deception is a particularly difficult sort of problem. To the extent that organizations are beset by self-deception—and most of them are—they can't see the problem. Most organizations are stuck in the box."

That claim hung in the air as Bud reached for his glass of water and took a drink. "By the way," he added, "the woman's name is Joyce Mulman."

"Who . . . what woman?"

"The person whose hand you refused. Her name is Joyce Mulman."

7   *People or Objects*

"How do you know her?" I asked worriedly. "And how'd you hear about what happened?"

Bud smiled reassuringly. "Don't be fooled by the distance between buildings. Word travels fast. I heard about it from a couple of your quality team leaders who were discussing it over lunch in the Building 5 cafeteria. It seems you made quite an impression."

I struggled to keep my composure and control my expression.

"As for knowing her," Bud continued, "I don't really, except that I try to know the names of as many people as I can around the company. It gets more difficult by the month with all of our growth, though."

I nodded, amazed that someone in Bud's position would worry about knowing the name of someone who was at Joyce's level in the company.

"You know those pictures we take for clearance badges?"

I nodded.

"Well, the executive team members receive copies of all those pictures, and we try to familiarize ourselves with, if not completely memorize, the faces and names of the people who join the company.

"I have found, at least with me," he continued, "that if I'm not interested in knowing a person's name, I'm probably not really interested in the person as a person. For me, it's a basic litmus test. Now, it doesn't necessarily work the other way around — that is, I can learn and know people's names and have them still be just objects to me. But if I'm unwilling even to try to remember someone's name, that itself is a clue to me that he or she is probably just an object to me and that I'm in the box. Anyway, that's why I know her—or at least how I know *of* her."

As Bud talked, my mind was taking inventory of the people in my division. I realized that of the 300 or so people in my part of the company, I knew only about 20 by name. *But I've been here only a month!* I said to myself in protest. *What more could you expect?* But I knew better. I knew that what Bud said about himself was true of me as well. The amount of time I had worked at Zagrum was a red herring. The truth was, I hadn't really *tried* to learn anyone's name. And as I thought about that now, it seemed clear that my lack of interest in as basic an issue as others' names was a pretty clear indication that I probably wasn't seeing them as people.

"I guess you think I really messed up," I said, my thoughts turning back to Joyce.

"It's not important what I think. What's important is what *you* think."

"Well, I'm kind of torn. On the one hand, I feel I owe Joyce an apology. But on the other hand, I still think she shouldn't have gone in that room and erased everything without checking first."

Bud nodded. "Do you suppose it's possible that you're right on both counts?"

"What? That I was wrong and right at the same time? How can that be?"

"Think of it this way," offered Bud. "You're saying that Joyce shouldn't just haul off and erase things that other people have written without finding out if that's okay first. Is that right?"

"Yes."

"That seems perfectly reasonable to me as well. And you're saying that the right thing in the situation was to tell her that she must never do that again. Is that right?"

"Yes, that's the way it seems to me."

"Me too," said Bud.

"Then what did I do wrong?" I asked. "That's exactly what I did."

"Yes, that *is* what you did," Bud agreed, "but here's the question: Were you in the box or out of the box when you did it?"

All of a sudden, a light went on for me. "Oh, I get it. It's not that I did the wrong thing necessarily but that I did what I did—maybe even the 'right' thing—in the wrong way. I was seeing her as an object. I was in the box. That's what you're saying."

"Exactly. And if you do what might on the surface be considered the right thing, but do it while in the box, you'll invite an entirely different and less productive response than you would if you were out of the box. Remember, people primarily respond not to what we do but to how we're *being*—whether we're in or out of the box toward them."

This seemed to make sense, but I wasn't sure it was realistic for the workplace.

"Is there something you're wondering about?" Bud asked.

"Not really," I said without conviction. "Well, I *am* struggling with one thing."

"Sure, go ahead."

"I'm just sitting here wondering how you can conduct a business seeing others as people all the time. I mean, won't you get run over doing that? I can see it applying to family life, for example, but isn't it a bit unrealistic to think that you have to be that way at work too, when you've got to be fast and decisive?"

"I'm glad you asked that," Bud said. "It was the next thing I wanted to talk about." He paused and then said, "First, I want you to think of Joyce. The way you handled the situation, I'd imagine that she won't ever be using your conference room again."

"Probably not."

"And since that's what you wanted to convey to her, you might think that your meeting with her was a success."

"Yeah, in a way I guess that's right," I said, feeling a bit better about what I'd done.

"Fair enough," Bud said. "But let's think beyond the conference room. Do you think that by being in the box when you conveyed your message, you invited in her *more* enthusiasm and creativity about her work or *less*?"

Bud's question caught me up short. All of a sudden, I realized that to Joyce Mulman, I was like Chuck Staehli. I remember being dressed down by Staehli, who seemed always in the box as near as I could tell, and I knew firsthand how demotivating it was to work with him as a result. To Joyce, I must seem no different from Staehli. The thought was terribly depressing.

"I guess that's right," I answered. "I might've solved the conference room problem but created other problems in its wake."

"It's worth thinking about," Bud agreed, nodding. "But your question actually goes to something deeper than that. I'll try to address it."

He stood up again and resumed his pacing. "Your question assumes that when we're out of the box, our behaviors are 'soft,' and when we're in the box, our behaviors are 'hard.' That's why you wonder, I take it, whether one can actually sustain a business being out of the box all the time. But let's think a little harder about that assumption. Is the distinction between being *in* the box and being *out of* the box a behavioral one?"

I thought about that for a minute. I wasn't certain, but it seemed like it might make a difference in behavior. "I'm not sure," I said.

"Let's look at the diagram," Bud said, pointing to what he had drawn on the board earlier. "Remember, this woman and I exhibited the same outward behaviors, but our experiences were completely different—I was *in* the box and she was *out*."

"Okay," I nodded.

"Here's an obvious question, but its implications are extremely important," he said. "Where on this diagram are behaviors listed?"

"At the top," I said.

"And where are the in-the-box and out-of-the-box ways of being listed?"

"Beneath that, at the bottom."

"Yes," Bud said, turning away from the board and toward me. "What's the implication of this?"

I didn't know what he was after and sat silently, groping for an answer.

"What I mean," Bud added, "is that this diagram suggests that there are two ways to do . . . what?"

I studied the diagram. Then I saw what he was getting at. "I see—there are two ways to do the behaviors."

"Right. So here's the question again: Is the distinction we're talking about fundamentally a distinction in behavior, or is it deeper than that?"

"It's deeper," I said.

Bud nodded. "Now, let's think of Lou again for a minute. How would you characterize his behavior toward me? Remember, in a public forum, in front of my colleagues, he took from me a responsibility I had failed to accomplish, even though I'd accomplished everything else he'd asked me to do. And then he asked me if I would ever let him down again. How would you characterize his behavior toward me—would you say it was soft or hard?"

"That would definitely be hard," I said, "*too* hard, even."

"Yes. But was he in the box or out of the box when he did it?"

"Out of the box."

"And how about you? How would you characterize your behavior toward Joyce—was it soft or hard?"

"Again, hard—perhaps too hard," I said, squirming slightly in my seat.

"You see," Bud said, as he walked back toward his chair across from me, "there are two ways to be hard. I can engage in hard behaviors and be either *in* the box or *out of* the box when I do them. The distinction isn't the behavior. It's the way I'm being when I am doing *whatever* I'm doing—be it soft *or* hard.

"Let's look at it another way," he continued. "If I'm out of the box, I'm seeing others as people. Fair enough?"

I nodded. "Yeah."

"Here's the question, then: Is the thing that a person needs always soft?"

"No, sometimes people need a little hard encouragement," I said with a wry smile.

"That's right. And your situation with Joyce is a perfect example. She needed to be told that it was wrong to erase other people's notes from the board, and passing on that kind of message could be thought of as behaviorally hard. The point is that it's possible to deliver just that kind of hard message and still be out of the box when doing it. But it can be done out of the box only if the person you are delivering the message to is a *person* to you. That's what it *means* to be out of the box. And notice—and here's why this is so important—whose hard message likely invited a more productive response, Lou's or yours?"

I thought again of how demotivating it was to work for Chuck Staehli and about how I probably had the same kind of influence on Joyce as Chuck had had on me. "Lou's, I'm afraid."

"That's the way it seems to me too," Bud said. "So regarding hard behavior, here's the choice: We can be hard and invite productivity and commitment, or we can be hard and invite resistance and ill will. The choice isn't to be hard or not, it's to be in the box or not."

Bud looked at his watch. "It's now 11:30, Tom. I have a proposal. If it's okay with you, I'd like to break for an hour and a half or so."

I was surprised by the time. It didn't seem like we'd been at this for two and a half hours, but I was grateful for the break all the same. "Sure," I said. "So we'll get going again at one o'clock, here?"

"Yes, that would be great. Now remember what we've covered so far: There's something deeper than behavior that determines our influence on others—it's whether we're in or out of the box. You don't know much about the box yet, but when we're in the box, our view of reality is distorted—we see neither ourselves nor others clearly. We are self-deceived. And that creates all kinds of trouble for the people around us.

"With that in mind," he continued, "I'd like you to do something for me before we get back together after lunch. I'd like you to think about the people here at Zagrum—both in and out of your department—and ask yourself whether you're in or out of the box toward them. And don't lump the people you're thinking about into an impersonal mass. Think of the individuals. You may be in the box toward one person and out of the box toward another at the same time. Think of the people."

"Okay, I will," I said as I started to stand up. "Thanks, Bud—this has been very interesting. You've given me a lot to think about."

"Not nearly as much as you'll have to think about by this afternoon," Bud said with a chuckle.

8 *Doubt*

The August sun was blazing overhead as I made my way back to the path that paralleled Kate's Creek. Although I had grown up in St. Louis and had lived for years on the East Coast, I had spent enough time in milder climates to become permanently uncomfortable with the humidity that accompanied Connecticut's summer heat. I was grateful to slip beneath the trees as I turned in the direction of Building 8.

For the exposure I was feeling on the inside, however, there was no cover. I was on completely unfamiliar ground. Nothing I had experienced in my career had prepared me for my meeting with Bud. But although I was feeling quite unsure of myself and was far less convinced that I was on the top of the Zagrum advancement heap than I had been just a few hours before, I also had never felt better about what I was doing. I knew there was something I had to do during this break—I just hoped that Joyce Mulman was around to allow me to do it.

"Sheryl, could you tell me where Joyce Mulman's desk is?" I asked my secretary as I walked past her and into my office. As I turned from putting my notebook on the table, I noticed that Sheryl was standing at my door, a worried look on her face.

"What's wrong?" she asked slowly. "Has Joyce done something again?"

Sheryl's words implied concern for me, but her manner betrayed her concern for Joyce, as if she wanted to warn Joyce of an impending storm if she had the chance. And I was surprised by the assumption, implicit in her question, that if I wanted to see someone, it must be because that person had done something wrong. My meeting with Joyce could wait for a minute. I needed to meet with Sheryl.

"No, nothing's wrong," I said. "Come in for a minute, though—there's something I want to talk to you about." Seeing her uncertainty, I said, "Please, take a seat." I walked around the desk and sat across from her.

"I'm new here," I began, "and you haven't had a lot of experience with me yet, but I want to ask you a question— and I need you to be absolutely candid with me."

"Okay," she said noncommittally.

"Do you like working with me? I mean, compared with others you've worked for, would you say I'm a good boss?"

Sheryl squirmed in her seat, obviously uncomfortable with the question. "Sure," she offered in an overly eager voice. "Of course I like working for you. Why?"

"I'm just wondering," I said. "So you like working for me?"

She nodded unconvincingly.

"But would you say you like working with me as much as others you've worked for?"

"Oh, sure," she said with a forced smile, looking down at my desk. "I've liked everyone I've worked for."

My question had put Sheryl in an impossible situation. It was supremely unfair. But I had my answer: She didn't like me much. The truth showed in her forced nonchalance and fidgeting discomfort. But I felt no ill will toward her. For the first time in a month, I felt sorry. I also felt a little embarrassed.

"Well, thank you, Sheryl," I said. "But I'm starting to feel that I've probably been kind of lousy to work with."

She didn't say anything.

I looked up and thought I noticed water forming in her eyes. Four weeks with her and I'd driven her to tears! I felt like the biggest heel. "I'm really sorry, Sheryl. Really sorry. I think I have some things to unlearn. I think I've been blind to some of the things I do to people. I don't know a lot about it yet, but I'm beginning to think about how I might sort of minimize others and fail to see them as people. You know what I'm talking about?"

To my surprise, she nodded knowingly.

"You do?"

"Sure. The box, self-deception, and all of that? Yes. Everyone here knows about it."

"Did Bud talk to you too?"

"No, not Bud. He meets personally with all the new senior managers. There's a class here that everyone goes through where we learn the same things."

"So you know about the box—seeing others as people or seeing them as objects?"

"Yes, and self-betrayal, collusion, getting out of the box, focusing on results, the four levels of organizational performance, and all the rest."

"I don't think I've learned any of those things yet. At least Bud hasn't mentioned them. What was that—self . . . ?"

"Betrayal," Sheryl said, filling in the gap. "It's how we get in the box in the first place. But I don't want to spoil what's coming. It sounds like you've only just started."

Now I *really* felt like a heel. It was one thing to treat another person as an object if she was as clueless to all these ideas as I had been, but knowing about the box, Sheryl had probably been seeing right through me the whole time.

"Boy, I've probably seemed like the biggest jerk to you, haven't I?"

"Not the biggest," she said with a smile.

Her wisecrack eased my mood, and I laughed. It was probably the first laugh between us in the four weeks we'd worked together, and in the ease of the moment, that seemed like a real shame. "Well, maybe by this afternoon I'll know what to do about it."

"Maybe you know more about it than you think you do," she said. "By the way, Joyce is on the second floor, next to the pillar marked '8-31.'"

When I passed by Joyce's cubicle, it was empty. *She's probably at lunch*, I thought. I was about to leave but then thought better of it: *If I don't do this now, who knows if I'll ever do it?* I sat down on an extra chair in the cubicle and waited.

The cubicle was plastered with pictures of two little girls about three and five years old. And there were crayon drawings of happy faces, sunrises, and rainbows. I might have been sitting in a day-care center except for the piles of charts and reports stacked all around the floor.

I wasn't sure what Joyce did in the organization—*my* organization—which seemed pretty pathetic to me at the moment, but from the look of all the stacks of reports, I gathered that she was a member of one of our product-quality teams. I was looking at one of the reports when she rounded the corner and saw me.

"Oh, Mr. Callum," she said in utter shock, stopping in her tracks, her hands to her face. "I'm sorry. I'm so sorry for the mess. It's not usually like this, really." She'd clearly been knocked off balance. I was the last person she probably ever expected to see in her cubicle.

"Don't worry about it. It's nothing compared to my office anyway. And please, call me Tom."

I could see the confusion in her face. She apparently had no idea what to say, or do, next. She just stood there at the entrance of her cubicle, trembling.

"I, uh, came to apologize, Joyce, for how I blew up at you about the conference room and all. That was really unprofessional of me. I'm sorry."

"Oh, Mr. Callum, I . . . I deserved it, I really did. I should never have erased your things. I've felt so bad about it. I've hardly slept in a week."

"Well, I think there probably was a way I could've handled it that wouldn't have left you sleepless."

Joyce broke out in an "Oh-you-didn't-have-to-do-that" smile and looked at the floor, pawing it with her toe. She'd stopped trembling.

It was 12:30. I had 20 or so minutes before I needed to make my way back over to continue with Bud. I was feeling pretty good and decided to call Laura.

"Laura Callum," said the voice on the other end.

"Hi," I said.

"Tom, I only have a second. What do you need?"

"Nothing. I just wanted to say hi."

"Is everything okay?" she said.

"Yeah, fine."

"You're *sure*."

"Yes. Can't I just call you to say hi without being interrogated?"

"Well, it's not like you ever call. There must be *something* going on."

"No, there's not. Nothing. Really."

"Okay, if you say so."

"Jeez, Laura. Why do you make everything so hard? I was just calling to see how you are."

"Well, I'm fine. And thanks for your concern, as always," she said, her voice dripping with sarcasm.

Everything that Bud had said that morning suddenly seemed far too naïve and simplistic. The box, self-deception, people or objects—all of those ideas might apply in some situations but not this one. Or if they did, who cared?

"Great. That's just great. Hope you have a nice afternoon," I said, matching her sarcastic tone and then some. "And I hope you're as cheerful and understanding with everyone there as you are with me."

The phone clicked dead.

No wonder I'm in the box, I thought as I hung up the phone. *Who wouldn't be, married to someone like that?*

I walked back to the Central Building full of questions. *First of all, what if someone else is in the box? What then? Like with Laura, it doesn't matter what I do. I called just to talk with her. And I was out of the box, too. But then, with one swift emotionless stroke, she cut me off at the knees—just like she always does. She's the one with the problem. It doesn't matter what I do. Even if I am in the box, so what? What could you expect?*

Okay, I had a couple of good experiences with Sheryl and Joyce. But what else are they going to do? I mean, I run the division. They have *to fall in line. And so what if Sheryl started to cry? Why should that be my fault? She has to be tougher than that. Anyone that weak deserves to cry—or at the very least, I shouldn't feel guilty if she does.*

My anger grew with each step. *This is a waste of time,* I thought. *It's all so Pollyannaish. In a perfect world, okay. But blast it, this is business!*

Just then, I heard someone call my name. I turned toward the voice. To my surprise, Kate Stenarude was cutting across the lawn toward me.

PART II

How We Get in *the Box*

9 *Kate*

I had met Kate just once. She'd been the final of my eight interviewers during the hiring process. I liked her instantly, as I'd since found out was common to nearly everyone in the company. Her story was in some ways the story of Zagrum, and like Zagrum's story, Kate's was freely passed along to new employees. She had joined the company fresh out of college some 25 years earlier, with a degree in history. One of the first 20 employees at Zagrum, she started as an order-fulfillment clerk. In those days, it seemed that Zagrum's future was in perpetual doubt. After five years, Kate, by then Zagrum's director of sales, left the company for a better opportunity, only to change her mind after a last-ditch personal appeal by Lou Herbert. Since that time, and until Lou's retirement, Kate had been second in command at Zagrum. At Lou's retirement, she was elevated to president and CEO.

"Hello, Tom," she said, extending her hand to me. "It's good to see you again. Is life treating you well?"

"Yeah, I can't complain," I said, trying to ignore for the moment both my surprise at meeting her and the disaster that was my home life. "How about you?"

"Never a dull moment, I'm afraid," she said with a chuckle.

"I can't believe you remember who I am," I said.

"What? Forget a fellow St. Louis Cardinals fan? Never. And besides, I'm coming to meet with you."

"With *me?*" I said incredulously, pointing at myself.

"Yes. Bud didn't say anything?"

"No. Or at least I don't think so. I think I would've remembered *that.*"

"Well, maybe he wanted it to be a surprise. I guess I ruined it for him," she said with a grin, apparently none too sorry. "I'm not often able to take part in these sessions, but I try to when my schedule allows. It's the thing I like most of all."

"Meeting hours on end talking about people's problems?" I said, trying to make a joke.

"Is that what you think this is about?" she said, a slight smile on her lips.

"No, I was just kidding. It's been pretty interesting, actually, although I have a few questions about it."

"Good. I'd expect you would. And you're with the right person. There's no one better than Bud to learn all this from."

"But I've got to say, I'm amazed that you and Bud are both going to spend your afternoon with me. I mean, isn't there any more important use of your time?"

Kate stopped suddenly. And just as suddenly, I wanted to rephrase my question.

She looked at me seriously. "This may sound funny, Tom, but there really isn't anything more important than this—at least not from our viewpoint. Nearly everything we do here at Zagrum—from our job formulations to our reporting processes to our measurement strategies—is built on what you're now learning."

What does this have to do with measurement? I wondered. I couldn't see the connection.

"But I wouldn't expect you to have a feel for the seriousness of it yet. You've only just started. I do think I know what you're saying, however," she continued, starting to walk again, although more slowly than before. "It does seem a little like overkill to have both Bud *and* me tied up with you this afternoon. And the truth is, it *is* overkill. I don't need to be there. Bud is much better at explaining it all than I am, anyway. It's just that I like this stuff so much that if I could — if I didn't have all the other responsibilities that normally tie me down — I'd be there every time. Who knows? One day I might yank the responsibility from Bud and take it for myself," she said, laughing at the thought. "Today is one of the rare times I can come, although I might have to slip out a little early."

We walked for a moment in silence. Then she said, "Tell me how it's been going so far."

"My work?"

"Your work . . . yes, but I really mean your experience *today*. How's it been going?"

"Well, other than being told that I'm in the box, it's going great," I replied, smiling as much as I could.

Kate laughed. "Yeah, I know what you mean. But don't take it too hard. Bud's in the box too, you know," she said with a gentle smile and a light touch to my elbow. "And so am I, for that matter."

"But if everyone's in the box anyway," I said, "including successful people like you and Bud, then what's the point?"

"The point is that although we're still sometimes in the box, and probably always will be to some extent, our success has come because of the times and ways that we at the company have been *out* of the box. This isn't about perfection. It's simply about getting better — better in systematic and concrete ways that improve the company's bottom line. That kind of leadership mentality — at every level of the organization — is what sets us apart.

"Part of the reason I come to these sessions when I can," she continued, "is to be reminded of some things. The box can be a pretty tricky place. You'll understand a lot more about that by the end of the day."

"But there's something I'm confused about right now, Kate."

"Only one thing?" she said, smiling, as we climbed the stairs to the third floor.

"Well, maybe more than one, but here's one for starters: If there really are two ways of being—the out-of-the-box way where I see people as people and the in-the-box way where I see others as objects—what makes you one way or the other in the first place?" I was thinking of Laura and how impossible she was. "I mean, I'm thinking of a situation where it's impossible to be out of the box toward someone. Really impossible."

It seemed like I should continue the thought, or the question, whichever it was, but I couldn't think of anything else to say, so I just stopped.

"I think maybe Bud should be in on that answer," she said. "Here we are."

10. *Questions*

"Hi Tom," Bud said warmly as we walked through the doors. "Did you have a good lunch?"

"It was too eventful for lunch, actually," I replied.

"Really? I look forward to hearing about it. . . . Hey, Kate."

"Hi, Bud," she said, walking over to the minifridge of juices. "Sorry I ruined your surprise."

"I didn't intend your coming as a surprise, actually. I just wasn't sure whether you'd be able to make it, so I didn't want to get Tom worked up for nothing. I'm glad you could come." He walked toward the conference table. "Let's all sit down and get to it. We're a little behind."

I went to the same chair I had sat in that morning, with my back to the window, near the middle of the conference table. As I did so, Kate, who was sizing up the room, suggested that we move closer to the whiteboard. Who was I to argue?

Kate sat in the seat nearest the board on the other side of the table, and I took the seat across from her, my back still to the window. She motioned Bud to sit between us at the head of the table, his back to the board. "Come on, Bud. It's your meeting."

"I was kind of hoping you'd take it over. You do this better than I do," he said.

"Oh, no I don't. I'll jump in now and then, but it's your show. I'm here to cheer you on . . . and to relearn a few things."

Bud sat down as directed, and he and Kate both smiled, obviously enjoying the friendly banter. "Well, Tom. Before we move into some new things, why don't you review for Kate what we've done so far."

"Okay," I said, trying to quickly collect my thoughts.

I reviewed for Kate what Bud had taught me about self-deception: how at any given moment we're either in or out of the box toward others; how, citing Bud's airplane examples, we can apparently do almost any behavior either in or out of the box, but that whether we're in or out makes a huge difference in the influence we have on others. "Bud's been suggesting," I continued, "that success in an organization is a function of whether we're in the box or not, and that our influence as leaders depends on the same thing."

"And I can't tell you how much I believe that," said Kate.

"I think I can kind of see it, too," I said, wanting to be agreeable. "But Bud also said that this issue of whether or not we're in the box is at the heart of most of the people problems we see in organizations. I must admit I'm not altogether sure about *that* yet. And on the way over here, you said that Zagrum's reporting and measurement systems grow out of all this, and I'm *really* in the dark about how that would be."

"Yeah, I'll bet you are," Bud said, looking pleased. "By the time we go home tonight, I think you'll be starting to have a feel for all of that. At least I hope so. But before we move forward, you mentioned something about a busy hour and a half since we last met. Anything that pertains to what we've talked about?"

I nodded and told them about Sheryl and Joyce. Bud and Kate seemed delighted. "That all went really well," I said. "But then . . . " Without thinking, I almost launched into my problems with Laura. I caught myself just in time. "Then I called someone," I said.

Bud and Kate waited expectantly.

"I don't want to get into it much," I said, trying to hide the fact that I was having trouble in my marriage. "It's sort of irrelevant to what we're doing here. But this particular person is pretty deep in the box, and all I have to do is talk with him and I'm in it, too. That's what happened when I called. I was out of the box, I'd just had these two good experiences, and I just wanted to call and see how he was doing. But he wouldn't let me do it. He wouldn't let me be out of the box. He just slammed me right back in. Under the circumstances, I think I did about as good a job as I could have done." I'd expected Bud or Kate to say something to this, but both remained silent, as if inviting me to continue. "It's no big deal, really," I continued, "it's just that it has me a little confused."

"About what?" asked Bud.

"About the whole box thing to begin with," I said. "I mean, if others keep putting us in the box, what can we do about it? I guess what I want to know is, how can you get out of the box when someone keeps putting you in it?"

At this, Bud stood up, rubbing his chin. "Well, Tom," he said, "we're certainly going to get to how we get out of the box. But first we have to understand how we get in it.

"Let me tell you a story."

11   *Self-Betrayal*

"Now at first you're going to think this is a silly story. It's not even a workplace story. We'll apply it to the workplace when we get a little more under our belts. Anyway, it's just a simple little story—mundane even. But it illustrates well how we get in the box in the first place.

"One night a number of years ago, when David was just an infant, I was awakened by his wailing cries. He was probably four months old or so at the time. I remember glancing at the clock. It was around 1:00 AM. In the flash of that moment, I had an impression or a sense or a feeling—a thought of something I should do. It was this: 'Get up and tend to David so that Nancy can sleep.'

"If you think about it, this sort of sense is very basic," he continued. "We're all people. And when we're out of the box and seeing others as people, we have a very basic sense about others—namely that, like ourselves, they have hopes, needs, cares, and fears. And on occasion, as a result of this sense, we have impressions of things to do for others—things we think might help them, things we can do for them, things we *want* to do for them. You know what I'm talking about?"

"Sure, that's clear enough," I said.

"This was such an occasion—I felt a desire to do something for Nancy. But you know what? I didn't act on it. I just stayed in the bed, listening to David wail."

I could relate. I'd waited out Todd and Laura plenty of times.

"You might say I 'betrayed' my sense of what I should do for Nancy," he said. "That's sort of a strong way to say it, but I just mean that in acting contrary to my sense of what was appropriate, I betrayed my own sense of how I should be toward another person. So we call such an act 'self-betrayal.'"

At that, he turned to the board to write. "Do you mind if I erase this diagram?" he asked, pointing at the diagram of the two ways of doing behavior.

"No, that's fine," I said. "I've got it."

In its place, in the top left corner of the board, he wrote the following:

"SELF-BETRAYAL"

1. An act contrary to what I feel I should do for another is called an act of "self-betrayal."

"Self-betrayal is one of the most common things in the world, Tom," Kate added, in an easy manner. "It might help to hear a few more examples." She looked at Bud. "Would you mind?"

"Please."

"Yesterday I was at Rockefeller Center in New York," she began. "I got into the elevator, and as the door started to close, I saw someone scurry around the corner and race toward the elevator. In that instant, I had a sense that I should catch the door for him. But I didn't. I just let it close, my last view being that of his outstretched, lunging arm. Have you ever had that experience?"

I had to admit I had and nodded sheepishly. "Or how about these: Think of a time when you felt you should help your child or your partner but then decided not to. Or a time when you felt you should apologize to someone but never got around to doing it. Or a time when you knew you had some information that would be helpful to a coworker, but you kept it to yourself. Or a time when you knew you needed to stay late to finish some work for someone but went home instead — without bothering to talk to that person about it. I could go on and on, Tom. I've done all of these, as I bet you have, too."

"Pretty much, yeah."

"They're all examples of self-betrayal — times when I had a sense of something I should do for others but didn't do it."

Kate paused, and Bud stepped in. "Now think about it, Tom. This is hardly a monumental idea. It's about as simple as it comes. But its implications are astounding. And astoundingly unsimple. Let me explain.

"Let's go back to the crying-baby story. Picture the moment. I felt I should get up so that Nancy could sleep, but then I didn't do it. I just stayed lying there next to Nancy, who also was just lying there."

As Bud was saying this, he drew the following in the middle of the board:

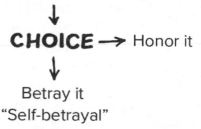

SENSE
Get up and tend to David so Nancy can sleep
↓
CHOICE → Honor it
↓
Betray it
"Self-betrayal"

"Now, in this moment, as I'm just lying there listening to our wailing child, how do you imagine I might've started to see, and feel about, Nancy?"

"Well, since she wasn't getting up, she may have seemed kind of lazy to you," I said.

"Okay, 'lazy,'" Bud agreed, adding it to the diagram.

"Inconsiderate," I added. "Maybe unappreciative of all you do. Insensitive."

"These are coming pretty easily to you, Tom," Bud said, adding my responses to the diagram.

"Yeah, well, I must have a good imagination, I guess," I said, playing along. "I wouldn't know any of this for myself."

"No, of course you wouldn't," said Kate. "Nor would you either, would you, Bud? The two of you are probably too busy sleeping to be aware of any of this," she said, chuckling.

"Aha, the battle is joined," laughed Bud. "But thank you, Kate. You raise an interesting point about sleeping." Turning back to me, he asked, "What do you think, Tom? Was Nancy really asleep?"

"Oh . . . maybe, but I doubt it."

"So you think she was faking it—pretending to sleep?"

"That'd be my guess, yes."

Bud wrote "faker" on the diagram.

"Hold on a minute, Bud," Kate objected. "Maybe she *was* asleep—and probably, from the sound of it, because she was so worn out from doing everything for *you*."

"Maybe so," Bud said with a grin. "But remember, whether she actually was asleep is less important right now than whether I was *thinking* she was asleep. We're talking now about my perception once I betrayed myself. *That's* the point."

"I know," Kate said, settling back into her chair. "I'm just having fun. If it were my example, you'd have plenty to pile on about."

"So from the perspective of that moment," Bud contin-ued, looking at me, "if she was just feigning sleep and letting her child wail, what kind of mom do you suppose I thought she was being?"

"Probably a pretty lousy one," I said.

"And what kind of wife?"

"Again, pretty lousy—inconsiderate, thinks you don't do enough, and so on."

Bud wrote both of these on the diagram.

"So, here I am," he said, backing away from the diagram and reading what he had written. "Having betrayed myself, we can imagine that I might've started to see my wife in that moment as lazy, inconsiderate, taking me for granted, insen-sitive, a faker, a lousy mom, and a lousy wife."

"Wow, Bud. Congratulations," said Kate, sarcastically. "You've managed to completely vilify one of the best people I know."

"I know. It's scary, isn't it?"

"I'll say."

"But it's worse than that, even," Bud said. "That's how I started to see *Nancy*. But having betrayed myself, how do you suppose I started to see *myself*?"

"Oh, you probably saw yourself as the victim—as the poor guy who couldn't get the sleep he needed," Kate replied.

"That's right," Bud said, adding "victim" to the diagram.

"And you would've seen yourself as hardworking," I added. "The work you had to do the next morning probably seemed pretty important to you."

"Good, Tom—that's right," Bud said, adding "hardwork-ing" and "important."

"How about this?" he asked after a pause. "What if I'd gotten up the night before? How do you suppose I would've seen myself if that had been the case?"

"Oh, as 'fair,'" Kate answered.

"Yes. And how about this?" he added. "Who is sensitive enough to hear the child?"

I had to laugh. All of this—the way Bud saw Nancy and the way he saw himself—seemed on the one hand so absurd and laughable but on the other hand so common. "Well, *you* were the sensitive one, obviously," I said.

"And if I'm sensitive to my child, then what kind of dad do I think I am?"

"A *good* one," Kate answered.

"Yes. And if I'm seeing myself as all of these," he said, pointing to the board—"if I see myself as 'hardworking,' 'fair,' 'sensitive,' a 'good dad,' and so on—then what kind of husband do I think I am?"

"A *really* good husband—especially putting up with a wife like the one you were thinking you had," Kate said.

"Yes," Bud said, adding to the list. "So look what we have."

SENSE
Get up and tend to David so Nancy can sleep

CHOICE → Honor it

Betray it
"Self-betrayal"

HOW I STARTED TO SEE **MYSELF**	HOW I STARTED TO SEE **NANCY**
• Victim	• Lazy
• Hardworking	• Inconsiderate
• Important	• Unappreciative
• Fair	• Insensitive
• Sensitive	• Faker
• Good dad	• Lousy mom
• Good husband	• Lousy wife

"Let's think about this diagram. For starters, look at how I started to see Nancy after I betrayed myself—as lazy, inconsiderate, and so on. Now think of this: Do these thoughts and feelings about Nancy invite me to reconsider my decision and do what I felt I should do for her?"

"Not at all," I said.

"What *do* they do for me?" Bud asked.

"Well, they justify your *not* doing it. They give you reasons to stay in bed and *not* tend to David."

"That's right," Bud said, turning to the board. He added a second sentence to his description of self-betrayal:

"SELF-BETRAYAL"

1. An act contrary to what I feel I should do for another is called an act of "self-betrayal."

2. When I betray myself, I begin to see the world in a way that justifies my self-betrayal.

"If I betray myself," Bud said as he backed away from the board, "my thoughts and feelings will begin to tell me that I'm justified in whatever I'm doing or failing to do."

He sat back down, and I thought of Laura.

"For a few minutes," he said, "I want to examine *how* my thoughts and feelings do that."

12   Characteristics of Self-Betrayal

"To begin with, think about this: When did Nancy seem worse to me, before I betrayed myself or afterward?"

"Afterward, for sure," I said, his question pulling me back to his story.

"Yes," said Bud, "and when do you suppose sleep seemed more important to me, before I betrayed myself or after?"

"Oh, I guess after."

"And when do you suppose other interests—like my work responsibilities the next morning, for example—seemed more pressing to me, before I betrayed myself or after?"

"Again, after."

Bud paused for a moment.

"Now here's another question: Take a look again at how I started to see Nancy. Do you suppose that in reality she's as bad as she seemed to me after I betrayed myself?"

"No, probably not," I said.

"I can vouch for Nancy," said Kate. "The woman described up there bears no resemblance."

"That's true," Bud agreed.

"Yeah, but what if she did?" I interjected. "I mean, what if she really *was* a lazy and inconsiderate person, and even a bad wife, for that matter? Wouldn't that make a difference?"

"That's a good question, Tom," Bud said, rising again from his chair. "Let's think about that for a minute."

He started to pace the length of the table. "Let's just say, for the sake of argument, that Nancy *is* lazy. And let's assume that she's generally inconsiderate too. Some people are, after all. Here's the question: If she was lazy and inconsiderate after

I betrayed myself, then she must've been lazy and inconsiderate before, right?"

"Yes," I answered. "If she's lazy and inconsiderate, she's lazy and inconsiderate. Before, after, it wouldn't matter."

"Okay, good," said Bud. "But if that's the case, then notice—I felt I should get up and help her *even though* she was lazy and inconsiderate. Before I betrayed myself, I didn't see her faults as reasons not to help her. I felt that way only *after* I betrayed myself, when I used her faults as justifications for my own misbehavior. Does that make sense?"

I wasn't sure. It seemed like it probably made sense, but the discussion made me uncomfortable because I had an example of this situation in my own house. Laura *was* inconsiderate, although perhaps not lazy. And it sure seemed to me that she was a pretty lousy wife. At least she had been recently. And it seemed like that was relevant to whether or not she deserved help from me. It was hard to want to help someone who showed no feelings for me. "I guess that makes sense," I said, still troubled and unsure about how and whether to express my concerns.

"Here's another way to think of it," Bud said, sensing my uncertainty. "Remember what we were just talking about. Even if Nancy really is lazy and inconsiderate, when do you suppose she would've seemed *more* lazy and inconsiderate to me—before I betrayed myself or after?"

"Oh yeah," I said, remembering the earlier point. "After."

"That's right. So even if she *is* lazy and inconsiderate, the truth is that in self-betrayal, I'm making her out to be more lazy and inconsiderate than she really is. And that's something *I'm* doing, not something she's doing."

"Okay, I get that," I said, nodding.

"So think about it," Bud continued. "Here I am in self-betrayal, and I think that I'm not getting up to help Nancy because of what she's doing to me—because she's lazy, inconsiderate, and so on. But is that the truth?"

I looked at the diagram. "No," I said, beginning to see the picture. "You *think* that's the truth, but it's not."

"That's right. The truth is, her faults seemed relevant to whether I should help her only *after I failed to help her*. I focused on and inflated her faults when I needed to feel justified for *mine*. After I betrayed myself, the truth was just the opposite of what I thought it was."

"Yeah, I guess that's right," I said, nodding my head slowly. This was getting pretty interesting. But I was still wondering how Laura fit into it.

"That's how Bud's view of Nancy was distorted," Kate added, "but consider how his view even of himself became distorted. Do you suppose that he's really as hardworking, important, fair, and sensitive as he was claiming himself to be? He was experiencing himself as a good dad and husband, for example, but in that moment, was he in actual fact *being* a good dad and husband?"

"No. That's right, he wasn't," I said. "At the same time that he was inflating Nancy's faults, he was also minimizing his own. He was inflating his own virtue."

"Yes," said Kate.

"So think about it," Bud said, jumping back into the conversation. "Was I seeing myself clearly after I betrayed myself?"

"No."

"How about Nancy? Was I seeing *her* clearly after I betrayed myself?"

"No. You weren't seeing anything very clearly," I said.

"So once I betrayed myself, my view of reality became distorted," Bud said in summary, turning toward the board. He added a third line to the description of self-betrayal:

"SELF-BETRAYAL"

1. An act contrary to what I feel I should do for another is called an act of "self-betrayal."

2. When I betray myself, I begin to see the world in a way that justifies my self-betrayal.

3. When I see the world in a self-justifying way, my view of reality becomes distorted.

"So, Tom," Bud said, after we'd paused to read what he'd written, "where was I after I betrayed myself?"

"Where *were* you?" I asked, trying to figure out the question.

"Think about it," he replied. "Before I betrayed myself, I simply saw something I could do to help Nancy. She was a person with a need that I felt I should fill. I saw the situation straightforwardly. But after I betrayed myself, my view both of her and of myself became distorted. I saw the world in a way that justified my failure. My perception became distorted systematically in my favor. When I betrayed myself, I became self-deceived."

"Oh, I see it," I said, enthusiastically. "So when you betrayed yourself, you entered the box. That's what you mean. That's the answer to your question of where you were—isn't it?"

"Exactly," he said, turning again and writing on the board. "Self-betrayal is how we enter the box."

"SELF-BETRAYAL"

1. An act contrary to what I feel I should do for another is called an act of "self-betrayal."

2. When I betray myself, I begin to see the world in a way that justifies my self-betrayal.

3. When I see the world in a self-justifying way, my view of reality becomes distorted.

4. So—when I betray myself, I enter the box.

"Based on this discussion, I think we should add a few summary elements to your diagram, Bud," Kate said, as she got up and walked toward the board.

"Sure, go ahead," he said, taking his seat.

First she drew a box around the description of Bud's experience after he betrayed himself. Then, to the side she wrote, "When I betray myself, I enter the box—I become self-deceived."

"Now," she said, turning to me, "I want to pull together and summarize from Bud's story four key characteristics of self-betrayal. And as I do it, I'm going to list them right here on this diagram.

"First of all," she said, "remember how after Bud betrayed himself, he made Nancy worse than she was?"

"Yeah," I nodded. "He inflated her faults."

"Exactly."

Kate added "Inflate others' faults" to the diagram.

"And what about Bud's *own* faults?" she said. "Did he see them straightforwardly after he betrayed himself?"

"No," I answered. "He sort of ignored his own faults and just focused on Nancy's."

"That's right." She added "Inflate own virtue" to the diagram.

"And do you remember what happened to the perceived importance of things such as sleep and fairness after Bud betrayed himself?" she asked.

"Yes. They seemed more important after he betrayed himself than they did before."

"That's right. After Bud betrayed himself, the perceived importance of anything in the situation that could provide justification for his self-betrayal became inflated—like, for example, the importance of sleep, fairness, and his responsibilities the next day."

Kate added "Inflate the value of things that justify my self-betrayal" to the diagram.

"Okay," she said. "One more, and then I'll sit down. When in this story did Bud start to *blame* Nancy?"

I looked at the diagram. "When he betrayed himself," I answered.

"That's right. He wasn't blaming her when he just felt he should help her. Only after he failed to help her."

She added "Blame" to the diagram.

"After I betrayed myself," Bud said, "consider how blame-filled my entire experience became. Those things on the diagram are all *thoughts* I had about Nancy, but consider what happened to my *feelings* toward her after I got in the box. For example, do you suppose I might have felt irritated?"

"Absolutely," I said.

"But notice," Bud said, drawing my attention to the diagram. "Did I feel irritated toward her when I just felt I should help?"

"No."

"And how about anger? Do you suppose I felt angry after I got in the box?"

"Oh yeah. Just look at the way you were seeing her. If my wife seemed that way, I'd be pretty mad at her." I was jolted by my own comment, because as I looked at the diagram, my wife *did* seem that way to me.

"You're right," Bud agreed. "I think I was plenty upset at what I viewed to be my wife's insensitivity to my situation. So my blaming didn't stop with my thoughts. In the box, my *feelings* were blaming, too. They said, 'I'm irritated because you're irritating, and I'm angry because you've done things to *make* me angry.' In the box, my *whole way* was blaming—both my thoughts and my feelings told me Nancy was at fault.

"And just to be clear here," he continued, "*was* Nancy to blame? Was I irritated and angry because of Nancy, like my irritation and anger were telling me? Were my thoughts and feelings telling me the truth?"

I thought for a moment. I wasn't sure. It seemed strange that feelings could lie, if that was what Bud was suggesting.

"Think about it this way," Bud went on, pointing to the board. "What's the only thing that happened in this story between the time that I wasn't irritated and angry and the time I was?"

I looked at the diagram.

"Your choice not to do what you felt you should do," I said. "Your self-betrayal."

"That's right. That's all that happened. So what caused my irritation and anger at Nancy?"

SENSE
Get up and tend to David so Nancy can sleep

↓

CHOICE → Honor it

↓

Betray it
"Self-betrayal"

↓

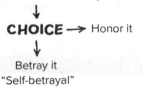

HOW I STARTED TO SEE **MYSELF**	HOW I STARTED TO SEE **NANCY**	When I betray myself, I enter the box—I become self-deceived
· Victim	· Lazy	**1.** Inflate others' faults
· Hardworking	· Inconsiderate	
· Important	· Unappreciative	**2.** Inflate own virtue
· Fair	· Insensitive	**3.** Inflate the value of things that justify my self-betrayal
· Sensitive	· Faker	
· Good dad	· Lousy mom	
· Good husband	· Lousy wife	**4.** Blame

"Your self-betrayal," I said, my voice trailing off as I be–came lost in the implications of this thought. *Really? Is that right?*

I looked again at the diagram. Before he betrayed himself, Bud saw Nancy, whatever her faults, simply as a person who could use his help. I understood that. But after he betrayed himself, she seemed very different to him. She didn't seem to *deserve* help anymore, and Bud thought he felt that way because of how *she* was being. But that wasn't true. The only thing that happened between the time that Bud felt irritated and angry and the time that he didn't was something that *Bud* did—his own self-betrayal—not something that Nancy did. So Bud's feelings *were* lying to him!

But that can't be my *case!* I screamed in my mind. *Laura really is a problem. I'm not just imagining it—and heaven knows I'm not making it up. I mean, there's no tenderness or caring in her at all. She's like a cool steel blade. And I know the pain of that blade. She uses it with skill. And Bud's telling me that's* my *fault? What about Laura? Why isn't it* her *fault?*

That thought caught me. *That's right,* I told myself. *Maybe it* is *her fault. She's the one who's betraying herself.* I started to feel better.

But wait, I argued with myself. *I'm blaming. That thought itself is a blaming. And blaming is something that Bud started doing* after *he betrayed himself, not before.*

Yeah, but so what? I fired back at myself. *If Laura's the one wielding the blade, I'm justified in blaming.*

But why do I need to feel justified?

Oh, blast it! Why am I questioning myself? I thought. *Laura's the one with the problem.*

But that's what Bud thought, too, I recalled.

I felt trapped between what I thought I knew and what I was learning. Either this stuff was all wet or I was. I was a mass of confusion.

Then I saw a way out.

13 Life in the Box

I looked up at the board again.

Yes! I cheered silently. *All of this trouble happened because Bud betrayed a feeling that he had for Nancy. But I rarely have those kinds of feelings for Laura. And the reason why is obvious — Laura is so much worse than Nancy. No one would feel they should do things for her given the way she is. My case is different. Bud got into trouble because he betrayed himself. I'm not betraying myself.* I sat back, satisfied.

"Okay, I think I get this," I said, preparing to ask my question. "I think I understand the idea of self-betrayal. Check me on it: As people, we have a sense of what other people might need and how we can help them. Right?"

"Yes," Bud and Kate said, almost in unison.

"And if I have that sort of sense and go against it, then I betray my own sense of what I should do for someone. That's what we call "self-betrayal." Right?"

"That's right. Yes."

"And if I betray myself, then I start seeing things differently — my view of others, myself, my circumstances — everything is distorted in a way that makes me feel okay about what I'm doing."

"Yes, that's right," Bud said. "You begin to see the world in a way that makes you feel justified in your self-betrayal."

"Okay," I said, "I understand that. And that's what you call 'the box.' I go into the box when I betray myself."

"Yes."

"Okay. But here's my question: What if I don't have a feeling that I betray? For example, what if when a child cries

I don't have a feeling or sense like the one you had? What if I just elbow my wife and tell her to get the kid? What you're saying is that it's not self-betrayal and that I wouldn't be in the box, right?"

Bud paused for a moment. "That's an important question, Tom. We need to think about it with some care. As for whether or not you'd be in the box, I wouldn't know. You'll have to think of situations in your life and decide for yourself. But there's something we haven't talked about yet that may help you with your question.

"So far we've learned how we get *in* the box. At this point we're ready to consider how we carry boxes with us."

"How we carry them with us?" I asked.

"Yes." Bud stood up and pointed at the diagram. "Notice that after I betrayed myself, I saw myself in certain self-justifying ways—for example, as 'hardworking,' 'important,' 'fair,' 'sensitive,' and the sort of person who's a 'good dad' and a 'good husband.' That's how I saw myself after I betrayed myself. But here's an important question: Was I lying there thinking of myself in these self-justifying ways *before* I betrayed myself?"

I thought about the question. "No, I wouldn't think so."

"That's right. These self-justifying ways of seeing myself arose in my self-betrayal—*when I needed to be justified.*"

"Okay, that makes sense," I said.

"But think about it," Bud continued. "The story of self-betrayal we've been talking about is just one simple example, and it happened many years ago. Do you think it's the only time I've ever betrayed myself?"

"I doubt it," I said.

"You can do more than doubt it," Bud said, chuckling. "I don't think I've ever gone a day without betraying myself in some way—and perhaps not even an hour. I've spent a *lifetime* betraying myself, as have you, Kate, and everyone else at Zagrum. And every time I've betrayed myself, I've seen myself in certain self-justifying ways—just like I did in the story we've been talking about. The result is that over time, certain of these self-justifying images become *characteristic* of me. They're the form my boxes take as I carry them with me into new situations."

At this, Bud added a fifth sentence to the list about self-betrayal:

"SELF-BETRAYAL"

1. An act contrary to what I feel I should do for another is called an act of "self-betrayal."

2. When I betray myself, I begin to see the world in a way that justifies my self-betrayal.

3. When I see the world in a self-justifying way, my view of reality becomes distorted.

4. So—when I betray myself, I enter the box.

5. Over time, certain boxes become characteristic of me, and I carry them with me.

I sat there trying to digest the meaning of all this, but I wasn't quite sure I understood.

"Let me show you what I mean. Let's take this self-justifying image right here," Bud said, pointing to "Good husband" on the diagram. "Let's imagine that over many self-betrayals, this self-justifying image has become characteristic of me. So as I move through my marriage and my life, I see myself as the sort of person who's a good husband. Fair enough?"

I nodded.

"Now consider this: It's Mother's Day, and near the end of the day my wife says in a hurt voice, 'I don't think you thought about me much today.'"

Bud paused, and I thought about Mother's Day at my own house a few months earlier. Laura had said almost the same thing.

"If I'm carrying a self-justifying image that says, 'I'm the sort of person who's a good husband,' how do you suppose I might start to see Nancy when she accuses me of not thinking about her? Do you suppose I might start to feel defensive and blame her?"

"Oh, absolutely," I said, thinking of Laura. "You'd blame her for failing to notice or give you credit for all the things you *do* do, for example."

"Yes. So I might blame her for being ungrateful."

"Or for even more than that," I added. "You might feel trapped by her. I mean, there she is, accusing you of being uncaring, when she's the one who hardly ever cares for *you*. It's hard to throw yourself into making her day wonderful when she herself never does anything that would make you want to do that in the first place." I stopped short as I felt the cool wind of embarrassment against my soul. Bud's story had transported me to my own troubles, and my indiscretion had given Bud and Kate a peek at the raw emotion I felt toward Laura. I cursed myself and resolved to stay more detached.

"That's right," Bud said. "I know exactly what you mean.

And when I'm feeling that way toward Nancy, do you suppose I might also inflate her faults? Might she seem worse to me than she really is?"

I didn't want to answer, but Bud waited. "Yeah, I suppose so," I said flatly.

"And notice something else," Bud continued. "As long as I'm feeling that way, will I ever seriously consider Nancy's complaint—that I hadn't really thought of her? Or will I be more likely to brush it off?"

I thought of an endless string of altercations with Laura. "You probably wouldn't question yourself much," I said finally, without much enthusiasm.

"Here I am," Bud continued, pointing to the board, "blaming Nancy, inflating her faults, and minimizing my own. So where am I?"

"I guess you're in the box," I answered, half-audibly, while my mind argued the point—*But what about Nancy? Maybe she's in the box, too. Why don't we consider that?* I suddenly started to feel very angry with this—all of it.

"Yes," I heard Bud say, "but notice—did I have to have a feeling that I betrayed in that moment in order to be in the box toward her?"

The question didn't quite register. "What was that?" I asked belligerently. The edge in my voice caught me by surprise, and I felt exposed once again. My resolution of detachment had held for all of a minute. "I'm sorry, Bud," I said, trying to recover, "I didn't quite catch the question."

Bud looked at me gently. It was clear that he'd noticed my anger, but he didn't seem put off by it. "My question was this: Here I was in the box toward Nancy—I was blaming her, inflating her faults, and so on—but did I have to have a sense that I betrayed in that moment in order to be in the box toward her?"

For some reason, this brief exchange and the focus required by Bud's question calmed me. I thought about his story. I couldn't remember him mentioning a sense that he betrayed. "I'm not sure," I answered. "I guess not."

"That's right. I didn't have to have a feeling that I betrayed in that moment in order to be in the box *because I was already in the box.*"

I must have looked a bit puzzled because Kate jumped in with an explanation. "Remember what Bud was just talking about, Tom. Over time, as we betray ourselves, we come to see ourselves in various self-justifying ways. We end up carrying these self-justifying images with us into new situations, and to the extent that we do, we enter new situations *already* in the box. We don't see people straightforwardly, as people. Rather, we see them *in terms of* the self-justifying images we've created. If people act in ways that challenge the claim made by a self-justifying image, we see them as threats. If they reinforce the claim made by a self-justifying image, we see them as allies. If they fail to matter to a self-justifying image, we see them as unimportant. Whichever way we see them, they're just objects to us. We're already in the box. That's Bud's point."

"Exactly," Bud agreed. "And if I'm already in the box toward someone, I generally won't have feelings to do things for them. So the fact that I have few senses to help someone probably isn't evidence that I'm out of the box. It may rather be a sign that I'm deep within it."

"So you're saying that if I generally don't have feelings to do things for someone in my life—say, for my wife, Laura— I'm probably in the box toward that person? Is that what you're saying?" I asked.

"No, not exactly," answered Bud, as he took his seat. "I'm suggesting that that's the way it generally is for *me* — at least for those I'm closest to in my life. Whether it's the same with you, toward Laura, for example, I don't know. You'll have to wrestle with that for yourself. But as a general rule, let me suggest this: If you seem to be in the box in a given situation but can't identify a sense you betrayed in that moment, that's a clue that you might *already* be in the box. And you may find it useful to wonder whether you're carrying around some self-justifying images that are feeling threatened."

"Like being the sort of person who's a good partner, for example?" I asked.

"Yes. Or the sort of person who's important or competent or hardworking or the smartest. Or being the sort of person who knows everything or does everything, or doesn't make mistakes or thinks of others, and so on. Almost anything can be perverted into a self-justifying image."

"What do you mean by *perverted*?"

"I mean that many self-justifying images are the in-the-box perversions of what would be great out of the box. For example, it's great to be a good partner. That's exactly what we should be for our partners. And it's great to think of others and to try to be as knowledgeable as we can be in whatever areas we work in. And so on. But these are the very things we're *not* being when we have self-justifying images about them."

"I'm not sure I understand," I said.

"Well," Bud said, standing again, "let's think about

self-justifying images for a minute." He resumed his pacing. "For example, certainly it's good to think of others, but who am I thinking of when I'm thinking of *myself* as the sort of person who thinks of others?"

"Yourself, I guess."

"Exactly. So my self-justifying image lies to me. It tells me I'm focused on one thing—in this case, others—but in having that image, I'm actually focused on myself."

"Okay, fair enough," I said, looking for holes in his logic. "But what about the one you mentioned about being smart or knowing everything? What's the problem with that?"

"Let's think about it. Let's say you have a self-justifying image that says you know everything. How do you suppose you'd feel toward someone who suggested something new to you?"

"I might find something wrong with his suggestion."

"Right. So would he keep coming to you with new ideas?"

"Probably not."

"And would you end up learning new things?"

"No, I guess not. Oh, I see your point," I said suddenly. "My self-justifying image about being learned can be the very thing that sometimes *keeps* me from learning."

"Yes. So if I have that self-justifying image, is knowing everything really what I'm most concerned about?"

"Not really. I guess your major concern is yourself—how you look."

"Exactly," Bud said. "That's the nature of most self-justifying images."

Bud continued, but I was no longer paying attention. I became lost in my own thoughts. *Okay, so I can carry my boxes with me. Maybe I have some of these self-justifying images that Bud is talking about. Maybe I'm in the box toward Laura. Maybe Laura is just an object to me generally. Okay. But what about* Laura? *All of this seems to be saying that I'm the one with the problem. But what about* her *problem? What about* her *self-justifying images? Let's talk about that!*

My anger was building again, when all of a sudden I became aware of it—and of something more: I was aware of the *hypocrisy* in my anger. For here I was, angry that Laura was in the box, but in my anger at her being in the box, *I* was in the box. I was angry at her for being like I was being! The thought caught me short, and Laura seemed different to me in an instant—not different in the sense that she no longer had problems but different in the sense that I saw myself as having problems, too. Her problems no longer seemed to excuse mine.

Kate's voice intruded on my thoughts. "Tom."

"Yeah?"

"Is this all making sense, Tom?"

"I think I understand it, yes," I said slowly. "I don't necessarily *like* it, but I understand it." I paused, still thinking of Laura. "I think I have some work to do."

It was an interesting moment. For the first time that afternoon, I was fully open to what Bud and Kate were sharing with me—open to the possibility that I had a problem. More than open, actually. I *knew* I had a problem, and in some ways a big one. Until that moment, I'd felt that giving in to the possibility that I had a problem would mean that I was the loser, that I'd been wrestled to the ground, that Laura had won. But now it didn't seem that way at all. I felt in a

91

strange way free and unencumbered. Laura didn't win, and I didn't lose. The world seemed much different from what it was the moment before. I felt hope. Amazingly, I felt hope in the moment I discovered I had a problem.

"I know what you mean," said Kate. "I have a lot of work to do myself."

"Me too," Bud said, nodding.

A moment or two passed in silence.

"We have one more thing to talk about," Bud said, "and then I want to turn our discussion back to business and see what all this means for Zagrum."

14   *Collusion*

"So far," Bud said, "we've been examining the internal experience of someone who's in the box. But as you can imagine, my box can have quite an impact on others.

"Think about it," he said, walking to the board. "Suppose this is me—in my box," he said, drawing a box with a stick figure in it.

"If I am here in my box, what am I communicating to others?"

"What are you *communicating*?"

"Yes."

"Well . . . you're blaming them, I guess."

"Exactly. And do you suppose other people are generally walking around saying to themselves, 'Gee, I really feel blameworthy today; I need someone to blame me'?"

I laughed. "Yeah, right."

"I don't think so, either," Bud said. "Most people are generally walking around thinking something like, 'Look, I'm not perfect, but doggone it, I'm doing just about as well as you could expect under the circumstances.' And since most of us have self-justifying images we're carrying around with us, most people are already in a defensive posture, always ready to defend their self-justifying images against attack. So if I'm in the box, blaming others, my blame invites them to do—*what?*"

"I guess your blame would invite *them* to be in the box."

"That's right," he said, drawing a second person in a box. "By blaming, I invite others to get in the box, and they then blame me for blaming them unjustly. But because I feel justified in blaming them while I'm in the box, I feel that *their* blame is unjust and blame them even more. Of course, while they're in the box, they feel justified in blaming me and feel that my further blame is unjust. So they blame *me* even more. And so on. So, by being in the box, I invite others to be in the box in response," he said, adding arrows pointing in both directions between the boxes. "And others, by being in the box in response, invite me to *stay* in the box, like this."

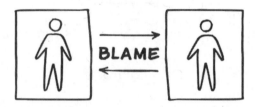

Then Bud added a sixth sentence to the principles he was writing about self-betrayal:

"SELF-BETRAYAL"

1. An act contrary to what I feel I should do for another is called an act of "self-betrayal."

2. When I betray myself, I begin to see the world in a way that justifies my self-betrayal.

3. When I see the world in a self-justifying way, my view of reality becomes distorted.

4. So—when I betray myself, I enter the box.

5. Over time, certain boxes become characteristic of me, and I carry them with me.

6. By being in the box, I provoke others to be in the box.

"You can put any flesh on these bones that you'd like," Kate said, pointing to the diagram, "and you'll see that when someone's in the box, the same pattern of mutual provocation and justification always emerges. Let me give you an example.

"I have an 18-year-old son named Bryan. And to be frank, he's been a struggle. One of the things that really bugs me is that he frequently gets home late."

I'd been so caught up in thinking about Laura that I'd nearly forgotten my troubles with Todd. The mere thought of him now, in response to Kate's comment about her boy, darkened my mood.

"Now imagine that I'm in the box toward Bryan. If I am, how do you suppose I'd likely see him and his getting home late?"

"Well," I said, "you'd see him as irresponsible."

"Okay, good," said Kate. "How else?"

"You'd think he's a troublemaker."

"And disrespectful," added Bud.

"Yes," agreed Kate. Then, pointing to the board, she asked, "Is it okay if I erase this blame diagram, Bud?"

"Sure."

Bud sat down and Kate walked to the board. She drew a summary of what we'd said. "Okay," she said, putting some finishing touches on the drawing. "So here we have it."

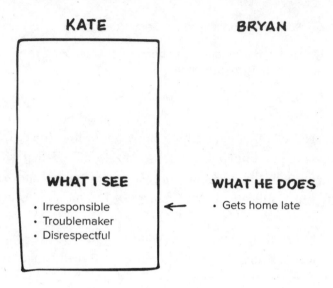

"Let's think about this situation. If I'm in the box and see Bryan as an irresponsible and disrespectful troublemaker, what sorts of things do you suppose I might do?"

"Well . . . " I began.

"You'd probably discipline him pretty severely," Bud interjected.

I nodded and added, "And you might start criticizing him a lot."

"Okay, good," Kate said, adding to the drawing. "Anything else?"

"You'd probably start hovering over his shoulder to make sure he was staying out of trouble," I said.

She added that to the drawing and stepped to the side. "Now let's suppose Bryan betrays himself—that he's in the box toward *me*. If he's in the box toward me, how do you suppose he might see me and my disciplining, criticizing, and hovering over his shoulder?"

"He'd probably see you as dictatorial," I said. "Or maybe unloving."

"And nosey," Bud added.

"Okay, 'dictatorial,' 'unloving,' and 'nosey,'" she repeated as she added to the drawing. "Good," she said. "Now look what we have."

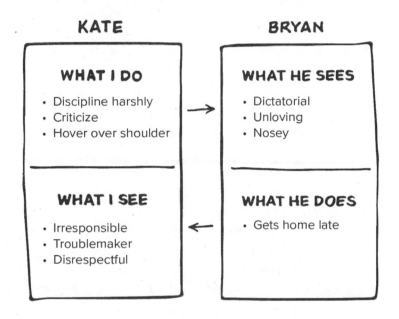

"If Bryan's in the box and seeing me as an unloving, nosey dictator, do you suppose he'll want to be home earlier or later?"

"Oh, later," I said. "*Far* later."

"In fact," Bud offered, "he'll be less likely to do *anything* the way you'd like him to do it."

"Yes," Kate agreed, drawing another arrow from Bryan's box to her own. "So around and around we go," she said, adding still more arrows between the boxes. "Think of it: We provoke each other to do more of what we say we don't like about the other!"

"Yeah, think about it, Tom," said Bud. "If you were to ask Kate in this situation what she wanted more than anything else in the whole world, what do you suppose she would tell you?"

"That she wanted Bryan to be more responsible, less trouble, and so on."

"Precisely. But what's the effect of what Kate does in the box? Does she invite more of what she says she wants?"

I looked at the diagram. "No. In fact, it looks like she invites more of what she says she *doesn't* want."

"That's right," Bud agreed. "She invites Bryan to do more of the very behavior that she says she hates."

This comment got me thinking about Todd, who frequently did things I didn't want him to do. I looked at the diagram again. On the one hand, Kate's role in this seemed crazy, as it looked like she was actually inciting more of the very behavior that she was complaining about. But on the other hand, what was she supposed to do? Just let her son get home late?

"But isn't Kate just doing what any parent would do in this situation?" I asked. "Sometimes you have to correct or punish children to get them to do what they need to do, don't you?"

"And do you suppose my being in the box invited Bryan to get home earlier?" Kate responded.

"Well, no," I said, "but—"

"Criticism is hard enough to receive even from someone who is out of the box, isn't it?" Kate interjected. "But from someone who's *in* the box—what are the chances of receiving *that* well?"

"I see. Probably not too good."

"And when do you think my discipline would be more appropriate to the circumstances and therefore more effective?" she asked. "When I'm in the box, inflating others' faults, or when I'm out of the box and seeing them clearly?"

I nodded. "When you're out."

"So you see, Tom, from within the box I end up undermining the effectiveness of everything I do—even if discipline in this case, for example, is exactly what Bryan needs. My box makes it nearly certain that I won't be able to invite in Bryan the changes I would like to see in him. And the problem isn't merely that the box makes me ineffective, it's that it makes me *destructive*. From within the box, I end up inviting more of the very thing that I'm complaining about, as well as other behaviors, as Bud pointed out, that I will hate just as much, if not more."

"But that's crazy," I said, after a moment's reflection. "Why would you—or anyone else, for that matter—ever do that? Why would we keep such a destructive cycle going?"

Kate paused for a moment, apparently collecting her thoughts. "I believe the answer to that, Tom, is that my box *needs* for it to continue."

"What?" I said reflexively. The answer didn't make any sense to me.

Kate smiled. "I know, it sounds absurd, doesn't it? Who would ever get themselves into a position where they actively invite others to continue treating them poorly, even miserably? Who would do that?"

"Exactly," I echoed, "who would do that?"

"And the answer, Tom, is that *I* would. And you would. And Bud would. And everyone else here at Zagrum would.

Whenever we are in the box, we have a need that is met by others' poor behavior. And so our boxes encourage more poor behavior in others, even if that behavior makes our lives more difficult."

"How? Why?" I asked.

"Let me answer those questions by telling you something that happened about a year ago in this situation with Bryan. On a particular Friday night, Bryan asked if he could use the car. I didn't want him to use it, so I gave him an unreasonably early curfew time as a condition—a time I didn't think he could accept. 'Okay, you can use it,' I said smugly, 'but only if you're back by 10:30.' 'Okay, Mom,' he said, as he whisked the keys off the key rack. 'Sure.' The door banged behind him.

"I plopped myself down on the couch, feeling very burdened and vowing that I'd never let him use the car again. The whole evening went that way. The more I thought about it, the madder I got at my irresponsible kid.

"I remember watching the 10 o'clock news, stewing over Bryan the whole time. My husband, Steve, was home, too. We were both complaining about Bryan when we heard the squeal of tires in the driveway. I looked at my watch. It was 10:29. And you know what?"

I was all ears.

"In that moment, when I saw the time, I felt a keen pang of disappointment.

"Now think about that for a minute," she continued after a short pause. "That night, I would have told you that the thing I wanted most was for Bryan to be responsible, to keep his word, to be trustworthy. But when he actually *was* responsible, when he did what he said he'd do, when he proved himself trustworthy, was I happy?"

"No." I shook my head in wonder at the thought. "You probably still would have been irritated, huh? You might have even gotten after him for squealing the tires."

"I'm ashamed to admit that I did something just as perverse," Kate replied. "After he came in the door—having made it in time, mind you—rather than thanking him, or congratulating him, or acknowledging him, I welcomed him with a curt, 'You sure cut it close, didn't you?'"

Kate sat down. "Notice—even when he *was* responsible, I couldn't *let* him be responsible." She paused. "I still needed him to be wrong."

I fidgeted as I thought of my own son.

"I would have told you at the time that I wanted a responsible son, but is that really what I wanted most, Tom?" she asked.

I shook my head. "It doesn't sound like it."

"That's right," she said. "When I'm in the box, there's something I need more than what I think I want most. And what do you think that is? What do I need most when I'm in the box?"

I repeated the question to myself. *What do I need most when I'm in the box? What do I need?* I wasn't sure.

Kate leaned toward me. "*What I need most when I'm in the box is to feel justified.* Justification is what my box eats, as it were, in order to survive. And if I'd spent my whole night, and really a lot longer even than that, blaming my son, what did I need from my son in order to feel 'justified,' to feel 'right'?"

"You needed him to be wrong," I said slowly, a knot forming in my stomach. "In order to be justified in blaming him, you needed him to be blame*worthy.*"

In that moment, I was transported back some 16 years. I was handed a little bundle by the nurse, and from that bundle, two cloudy eyes looked up toward my face. I was completely unprepared for what he would look like at birth. Bruised, misshapen, and grayish, he was a funny-looking kid, and I was his daddy.

I had been blaming Todd almost from that day. He was never smart enough, never coordinated enough. And he was always in the way. Since he started school, he had been in constant trouble. I didn't remember ever feeling proud when anyone realized he was my son. He'd never been good enough.

Kate's story scared me to death. I asked myself, *What must it be like to be the son of someone for whom you can never be good enough? And if Kate's right, then there's a sense in which I can't let him be good enough. I need him to be a problem in order to feel justified in always seeing him as a problem.* I felt sick, and I tried to push Todd out of my mind.

"That's exactly right," I heard Kate say. "Having spent the evening accusing Bryan of being a disappointment, I *needed* him to be a disappointment *so that I would be justified in accusing him.*"

We sat for a moment in thought.

Finally, Bud broke the silence. "Kate's story raises for me an astonishing point, Tom. And that is, when I'm in the box, I need people to cause trouble for me—*I actually need problems.*"

As incredible as that sounded, it rang true.

Bud rose from his chair. "Remember when you asked me this morning whether you can actually run a business being out of the box all the time? You said it seemed like you'd get run over if you were out of the box all the time, seeing people as people."

"Yeah, I remember."

"And then we talked about how that question is misguided, because you can do almost any behavior—'soft,' 'hard,' whatever—either in the box or out of the box. Do you remember?"

"Yes."

"Well, now we can say more about your question. It's an important question. Let's consider it in light of what Kate has just taught us. Think of it this way: Who *needs* to be run over—the person who is *in* the box or the person who is *out?*"

"The person *in* the box," I said, amazed by the implication.

"That's right. Out of the box I get no mileage whatsoever in being run over. I don't need it. And what's more, I'm usually not doing anyone a favor by letting them run over me. *In* the box, on the other hand, I get what I most need when I'm run over: I get my justification. I get my proof that the person running over me is just as bad as I've been accusing him or her of being."

"But in the box, you don't *really* want to be run over, do you?" I asked. "I mean, that's kind of strange. Kate's story got me thinking about my son, Todd. Laura and I feel like we get run over sometimes, but I don't think either of us really *wants* that."

"That's true," Bud responded. "We're not saying that in the box we *enjoy* problems. Far from it; we hate them. In the box, it seems like there's nothing we would want more than to be out from under them. But remember, when we're in the box, we're self-deceived—we're blind to the truth about others and ourselves. And one of the things we're blind to is how the box itself undercuts our every effort to obtain the outcomes we think we want."

Bud walked over to the board. "Think about Kate's story again for a moment." He pointed at the diagram. "Notice how her blaming from within the box provokes Bryan to be irresponsible, and then, when he *is* irresponsible, she takes that as justification for having blamed him in the first place for being irresponsible! Likewise, Bryan's blaming provokes Kate to be on his case, and then, when she *is* on his case, he takes that as justification for having blamed her in the first place for being on his case! By the simple fact of being in the box, each helps to create the very problems he or she blames the other for."

"In fact, Tom," Kate added, "Bryan and I provide each other with such perfect justification, it's almost as if we *colluded* to do so. It's as if we said to each other, 'Look, I'll mistreat you so that you can blame your bad behavior on me if you'll mistreat me so that I can blame my bad behavior on you.' Of course, we didn't ever say that to each other, or even think it, for that matter. But our mutual provocation and justification seem so perfectly coordinated, it *looks* like we did. For this reason, when two or more people are in their boxes toward each other, mutually betraying themselves, we often call it 'collusion.' And when we're in collusion, we actually collude in condemning ourselves to ongoing mutual mistreatment!"

"And we do this," Bud jumped back in, "not because we like being mistreated but because we're in the box, and the box *lives* on the justification it gets from our being mistreated. So there's a peculiar irony to being in the box: However bitterly I complain about someone's poor behavior toward me and about the trouble it causes me, I also find it strangely *delicious*. It's my proof that others are as blameworthy as I've claimed them to be—and that I'm as innocent as I claim *myself* to be. The behavior I complain about is the very behavior that justifies me."

Bud placed both hands on the table and leaned toward me. "So simply by being in the box," he said slowly and earnestly, "I provoke in others the very behavior I say I hate in them. And they then provoke in me the very behavior they say they hate in me."

Bud turned and added another sentence to the principles about self-betrayal:

"SELF-BETRAYAL"

1. An act contrary to what I feel I should do for another is called an act of "self-betrayal."

2. When I betray myself, I begin to see the world in a way that justifies my self-betrayal.

3. When I see the world in a self-justifying way, my view of reality becomes distorted.

4. So—when I betray myself, I enter the box.

5. Over time, certain boxes become characteristic of me, and I carry them with me.

6. By being in the box, I provoke others to be in the box.

7. In the box, we invite mutual mistreatment and obtain mutual justification. We collude in giving each other reason to stay in the box.

"Once in the box," Bud said, backing away from the board, "we give each other reason to *stay* in the box. We do this not only by mistreating the other person directly, by the way, but also by how we might begin to talk about or gossip about that person with others. The more people we can find to agree with our side of the story, the more justified we will feel in believing that side of the story. I might recruit my spouse to join with me in blaming my son, for example, or I might gossip about others in order to gather allies at work in my collusion against another person or department. And so on. Whether at home or at work, boxes want to spread in order to gather additional justification. And with every mistreatment—direct and indirect—we give each other further justification for staying in the box. That's the grim reality."

I slumped in my chair, suddenly aching for my boy.

"Now look, Tom," Bud said, sitting back down. "Think about how self-betrayal, and everything we've been talking about, explains the self-deception problem—the problem of being unable to see that I have a problem. To begin with, when I'm in the box, who do I think has the problem?"

"Others."

"But when I'm in the box, who, in fact, has the problem?"

"You do," I answered.

"But what does my box provoke in others?" he asked.

"It provokes them to behave badly toward you."

"Yes. In other words, my box provokes *problems* in others. It provokes what I take as proof that I'm not the one with the problem."

"Yeah, that's right," I agreed.

"So what will I do if anyone tries to correct the problem they see in *me*?"

"You'll resist them."

"Exactly," he said. "When having a problem, I don't think I have one. I think *others* are responsible." He paused for a moment and then said, "So here's the question: So what?"

So what? I repeated to myself. "What do you mean, 'So what?'"

"I mean just that," Bud answered. "Why should we care about any of this at Zagrum? What does it have to do with work?"

15 Box Focus

"It has *everything* to do with work," I said, surprised by the strength of my opinion.

"How?" Bud asked.

"How?" I replied.

Bud waited for an answer.

"Well, to begin with," I said, "nearly everyone at work is in the box, as near as I can tell. At least nearly everyone at Tetrix was."

"So what?"

"So what?" I repeated in surprise.

"Yeah, so what?" he said.

"Well, if we're in the box, we'll be inviting others to be in the box, too, and we'll end up with all kinds of conflict that gets in the way of what we're trying to do."

"Which is what?" Bud asked.

I hesitated, unsure of what Bud meant.

"You just said that all of that conflict would get in the way of what we're trying to do," Bud continued. "So my question is, what is it we're trying to do?"

"Trying to be productive, I suppose."

"Ah," Bud said, as though he had finally found what he was looking for. "So the box gets in the way of our achieving *results.*"

"Yes," I agreed.

"Let's think about how it does that," he said. "There are actually two main reasons why the box undercuts results. The first is what Kate has just taught us. When we're in the box, what motivates us most is the need for justification, and what will bring us justification is very often at odds with what is best for the organization. Does that make sense?"

I nodded, thinking as I did so that this was true whether the organization was a company or a family.

"Here at Zagrum, we use the term '*what*-focus' to describe whatever a person is focused on achieving. Out of the box, my what-focus at work is results. In the box, by contrast, my what-focus is justification. That's the first reason why the box always undercuts results."

That made sense. "What's the second reason?" I asked.

"It has to do with my '*who*-focus' when I'm in the box," Bud answered.

"You're focused on yourself when you're in the box, aren't you?" I said.

"Exactly, Tom, and as long as I am focused on myself, I can't fully focus either on results or on the people to whom I am to be delivering those results. In fact, if you think about it, many of the people typically described as being results-focused are anything but that. In the box, they value results primarily for the purpose of creating or sustaining their own stellar reputations—their who-focus is themselves. And you can tell because they generally don't feel that other people's results are as important as their own. Think about it—most people aren't nearly as happy when other people in the organization succeed as they are when they themselves do. So they run all over people trying to get only their *own* results—with devastating effects. They might beat their chests and preach focusing on results, but it's a lie. In the box, they, like everyone else, are just focused on themselves. But in the box, they, like everyone else, can't see it."

"It's even worse than that," Kate added. "Because, remember, in the box we provoke others to get in the box—both with us and against us. We and our allies withhold information, for example, which gives others reason to do the same. We try to control others, which provokes the very resistance that we feel the need to control all the more. We withhold resources from others, who then feel the need to protect resources from us. We blame others for dragging their feet and in so doing give them reason to feel justified in dragging their feet all the more. And so on.

"And through it all we think that all our problems would be solved if Jack wouldn't do this or if Linda wouldn't do that or if XYZ department would just straighten up or if the company would get a clue. But it's a lie. It's a lie even if Jack, Linda, XYZ department, and the company *need* to improve, which they surely do. Because when I'm blaming them, I'm not doing it because they need to improve; I'm blaming them because their shortcomings justify *my* failure to improve.

"So," she continued, "one person in an organization, by being in the box and failing to focus on results, provokes his or her coworkers to fail to focus on results as well. Collusion spreads far and wide, and the result is that coworkers position themselves against coworkers, workgroups against workgroups, departments against departments. People who came together to help an organization succeed actually end up delighting in each other's failures and resenting each other's successes."

"That's really crazy," I said in amazement. "But I see just what you're talking about all the time. Tetrix was full of those kinds of situations."

"Yes. Think about it," Bud said. "When were you most happy—when Chuck Staehli succeeded, or when he failed?"

The question caught me off guard. I had meant that I'd seen this in *others* all the time. Staehli *really was* a problem. I wasn't just making that up. And he created all kinds of trouble—conflict, poor teamwork, and so on. "I, uh, I . . . I don't know," I offered weakly.

"Well, you might think about it a little. When dealing with germs, the mere fact that someone else is sick doesn't mean that I'm *not* sick. In fact, when I'm surrounded by sick people, chances are greater that I will get sick myself."

He paused and looked at me for a moment. "Remember Semmelweis?"

I nodded. "The doctor who discovered the cause of the high mortality rate in the maternity ward."

"Yes. In his case, it was the doctors themselves—the people who focused on the sicknesses and problems of *others*—that spread the disease. As a result, childbed fever, with its various symptoms, spread unchecked, claiming victim after victim. All because of a single germ no one knew about—most especially those who carried it."

Bud stood up and moved to the board. "What happens in organizations is analogous. Let me show you what I mean."

16   *Box Problems*

"Do you remember my experience in San Francisco?" Bud asked.

"Yeah."

"Remember the problems I had there? How I wasn't engaged, wasn't committed, and was making things more difficult for others?"

"Yeah, I remember."

Bud erased everything that had been written next to the self-betrayal diagram. Then he wrote the following:

Lack of commitment
Lack of engagement
Troublemaking

"Okay, here are a few of the problems I had in San Francisco," he said, as he stepped back from the board. "My 'symptoms,' as it were. But let's add as many kinds of problems to this list as we can. What are some other common people problems in organizations?"

"Conflict," I said. "Lack of motivation."

"Stress," Kate added.

"Poor teamwork," I said.

"Hold on a minute," said Bud, writing furiously. "I'm trying to get them all up here. Okay, go ahead. What else?"

"Backbiting, alignment problems, lack of trust," Kate said.

"Lack of accountability," I offered. "Bad attitudes. Communication problems."

"Okay, good," Bud said, finishing the last few. "That's a good enough list. Now let's take a look and compare it with the story right over here where I failed to get up and tend to my child."

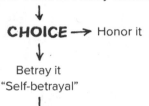

SENSE

Get up and tend to David so Nancy can sleep

↓

CHOICE → Honor it

↓

Betray it
"Self-betrayal"

↓

HOW I STARTED TO SEE **MYSELF**	HOW I STARTED TO SEE **NANCY**
· Victim	· Lazy
· Hardworking	· Inconsiderate
· Important	· Unappreciative
· Fair	· Insensitive
· Sensitive	· Faker
· Good dad	· Lousy mom
· Good husband	· Lousy wife

Lack of commitment
Lack of engagement
Troublemaking
Conflict
Lack of motivation
Stress
Poor teamwork
Backbiting/bad attitudes
Misalignment
Lack of trust
Lack of accountability
Communication problems

"Notice: Did I have a commitment or engagement problem after I betrayed myself?"

"Yes," I answered.

"But how about *before*? Did I have a commitment or engagement problem when I just had the feeling to get up and tend to David so that Nancy could sleep?"

"No," I said.

"How about making things more difficult for others? Was I making things more difficult for Nancy when I just had the feeling to help her?"

"No," I answered, "only after you betrayed yourself."

"That's right. And how about conflict—and stress? When do you suppose I was more stressed—when I just felt I should help Nancy or after I betrayed myself and was inflating the importance of the things I had to do the next morning?"

"Oh, after you betrayed yourself, for sure. Same with conflict. You weren't in conflict with Nancy before you betrayed yourself, only after."

"That's right," Bud agreed. "You can go down all of these people problems, and what you'll find is that they all existed after I betrayed myself but not before."

Bud paused, giving me a chance to look at the list and see for myself. Then he asked, "Which means what?"

"I'm not sure I know what you mean."

"Well, I had all of these people problems after I betrayed myself but not before. Which means what?"

"Which means . . . *oh.* Which means that they were caused by your self-betrayal," I finally said.

"Exactly, Tom. I didn't have those problems before I betrayed myself, only after. So the solution to the self-betrayal problem *is* the solution to all of those people problems."

Bud paused again, giving me time to digest the idea. Then he continued, "Remember how I said that, like Semmelweis's medical discovery, the solution to the self-deception problem amounts to a sort of unifying theory—a theory that shows that the various disparate problems we call 'people problems' really all have the same cause?"

"Yeah, I remember."

"Well, here's what I meant. Right here," he said, pointing to the diagram. "This simple story shows how it happens. Self-betrayal is the germ that creates the disease of self-deception. And, like childbed fever, self-deception has many different symptoms—from lack of motivation and commitment to stress and communication problems. Organizations die, or are severely crippled, by those symptoms. And that happens because those who carry the germ don't know they're carrying it."

I thought about the import of that for a moment, studying the diagram. "But is it always the same in business? I mean, after all, your example is about failing to get up to tend to a baby. That's not what's happening at work."

"That's true," he said. "You're right that the people at work aren't betraying themselves quite this way—no one is failing to tend to a baby. However, a lot of people are failing to do things for coworkers that they feel they should do, and they feel justified every time that happens, just like in this example. Every time we betray ourselves, we go in the box, and it doesn't matter whether we betray ourselves at home, at work, at the store, or wherever. The box—self-deception—will itself cause all the same kinds of problems in every one of those situations that it caused in this one.

"But there's something else," he continued. "There's a particular self-betrayal that almost everyone engages in at work to one degree or another, a self-betrayal concerning the very purpose of what we were hired to do—to focus on helping the organization and its people to achieve results. The key to solving most of the people problems that afflict organizations is in discovering how we can solve this central workplace self-betrayal."

"So how *do* you?" I asked eagerly.

"Ah, we're not quite ready to understand that yet. We have a few more ideas to consider first. But maybe we should take a break before we get to it."

Kate glanced at her watch. "I'm afraid I'm going to have to leave, guys. I have a 4:30 with Howard Chen. I wish I didn't have to. Tom," she said, rising from her chair and extending her hand to me, "it's been a real pleasure spending this time with you. I appreciate how seriously you're taking this. As I said before, there's nothing more important to us around here than what you're now learning. It's Zagrum's number one strategic initiative. You'll understand what that means as you get into what comes next."

"What do you think?" she said, turning to Bud. "Are you going to try to finish up the basics tonight?"

"If so, we'll be going a little late. Tom and I will have to talk about it."

"Sounds good," Kate said as she started for the door. "By the way, Tom," she said, turning back to me, "I *left* Zagrum once. It was a very different company then."

"Why did you leave?" I asked.

"Because of Lou Herbert."

That wasn't the answer I expected. "Really? I thought you and Lou were really tight."

"Not in the early days. Lou wasn't tight with anybody then. A lot of good people left."

"Then why'd you come back?"

"Because of Lou," she said.

I was confused. "What do you mean?"

"Lou found this material—the material you're learning now—and it transformed him. And in transforming *him*, it transformed the company. When he came to see me, he came to apologize, and he came with a plan. I've worked for Zagrum twice, but it might as well have been two different companies. You're learning about the need to apologize, like Lou. And you'll soon learn about the plan that follows from it. As I told you before, everything we do here is built on what you're learning. It's what makes this place tick."

She paused. "We're glad you're part of the team, Tom. You wouldn't be here unless we believed in you."

"Thanks," I replied.

"And thank *you*, Bud," she said, turning in his direction. "You never cease to amaze me."

"What are you talking about?" he asked, chuckling.

"I'm talking about what you mean to the company and the people in it. You're just like Lou became after he got his act together. You're Zagrum's secret weapon."

Kate smiled and headed toward the door. "Anyway, thanks," she said as she walked out. "And keep rooting for the Cardinals—both of you. Yes, even you, Bud," she said, responding to his frown. "Heaven knows, they need the help."

"Wow," I said to no one in particular, after Kate left. "I can't believe she took all that time to be with me today."

"Believe me," said Bud, "you don't know the half of it. She has tremendous demands on her time. But she comes whenever she can. And she comes because what we're now embarked on produces more results for this company than any other single thing we do. Her attendance is her way of saying, 'We're serious about this. And if you aren't, you won't stay long.'"

Bud patted me on the back. "It's the same thing for me, Tom. People who persist in being in the box don't make it here, and that's no less true of me than it is of you. We're in this together." He chuckled reassuringly. All I could think of, however, was Todd and Laura.

"Well, Tom," he said, signaling a change in topic, "we have a decision to make. We have a few more hours to go before we're through with the basics. And we can either finish tonight or meet again tomorrow, if that's possible for you."

I thought about my schedule. I had a full afternoon but could clear my morning schedule. "I think I'd prefer tomorrow morning."

"Good enough. Let's say 8:00 AM. And if I can arrange it, I might even have a surprise for you."

"A surprise?"

"Yeah. If we're lucky."

The warm August wind blew through my hair as I turned my convertible from Long Ridge Road east onto Merritt Parkway. I had a wife and son who needed some attention, perhaps even some apologies. I hardly knew where to begin. But I knew that Todd liked working on cars—an interest I had ridiculed whenever I could, out of fear that "Tom Callum's boy" would grow up to be a mechanic. And I also knew that Laura hadn't had a meal prepared for her in months. I had decided to pick up items for a barbecue, and I was feeling the desire to learn a thing or two about tuning engines.

For the first time in years, I was in a hurry to get home.

PART III

How We Get out of the Box

17   *Lou*

It was 8:15 AM, and Bud wasn't in the conference room yet. I was starting to wonder if I'd heard him correctly when the doors burst open and into the room walked an elderly gentleman.

"Tom Callum?" he said with a hearty smile, extending his hand.

"Yes."

"Glad to meet you. My name's Lou. Lou Herbert."

"Lou Herbert?" I said in astonishment.

I'd seen pictures of Lou and some old video, but his presence was so unexpected that I never would have recognized him without his introduction.

"Yes. Sorry for the shock. Bud's on his way. He's just checking on a couple of things for a meeting we have this afternoon."

I was dumbstruck. No words came to mind, so I just stood there nervously.

"You're probably wondering what I'm doing here," he said.

"Well, *yes*, as a matter of fact."

"Bud called last night and asked if I could join you guys this morning. He wanted me to explain a few things about my history here. I was coming over today anyway for this afternoon's meeting. So here I am."

"I don't know what to say. It's incredible to meet you. I've heard so much about you."

"I know. It's almost like I'm already dead, isn't it?" he said with a grin.

"Yeah, I guess it kind of is," I said, chuckling, before I knew what I was saying.

"Look, Tom, go ahead, sit. Bud asked me to get started with you before he arrives." He gestured toward a seat. "Please."

I sat in my familiar chair from the afternoon before, and Lou took the seat across from me.

"So how's it been going?"

"You mean yesterday?"

"Yes."

"It was quite an amazing day, actually. Quite amazing."

"*Really?* Tell me about it," he said.

Although I'd been with Lou for only a minute or two, my nervousness had evaporated. His kindly eyes and gentle demeanor reminded me of my dad, who had died 10 years earlier. I felt completely comfortable in his presence and found myself wanting to share my thoughts with him as I used to with my father.

"Well," I said, "I hardly know where to begin. I learned a lot yesterday. But let me start with my boy."

Over the next 15 minutes or so, I told Lou about the best night I'd had with Laura and Todd in at least five years. It was a night that was extraordinary only because I simply enjoyed being with them without anything extraordinary happening to make me enjoy it. I cooked, I laughed, I had my son teach me how to tune up the car. For the first time in I didn't know how long, I enjoyed and felt grateful for my family. And for the first time in a long time, I went to bed with no hard feelings toward anyone in my home.

"What did Laura think of it all?" Lou asked.

"I don't think she knew what to think. She kept asking me what was going on until I finally had to tell her about what I learned yesterday."

"Oh, so you tried to teach her?"

"Yeah, and it was a disaster. I think it took me only a minute or so to have her thoroughly confused. 'The box,' 'self-betrayal,' 'collusion'—I butchered the ideas so badly, I couldn't believe it."

Lou smiled knowingly. "I know what you mean. You hear someone like Bud explain all this and it seems like the simplest thing in the world, but try to do it yourself and you quickly realize how subtle it all is."

"That's true. I think my explanations probably created more questions than they answered. But she tried to understand anyway."

Lou listened intently, his eyes creased with kindness. And although I couldn't be sure, I thought I saw approval in them as well.

"You might check with Bud to see if this is still going on," Lou said, "but in the past, a couple of times a year we put on evening-long training events where interested family members could come and learn these ideas. It used to mean a lot to everybody that the company would do that for them. If it's still going on, Laura might really like it."

"Thanks. I'll check, for sure."

Just then, the door swung open and in walked Bud.

"Tom," he said, exasperated, "sorry I'm late. I had a few last-minute preparations for the meeting with the Klofhausen group this afternoon. As usual, there aren't enough last minutes."

He set his briefcase down and took the seat between Lou and me at the head of the table. "Well, Tom, we got lucky."

"What do you mean?"

"I mean Lou—he's the surprise I was hoping for. Lou's story is the story of how this material has transformed Zagrum, and I wanted him to share it with you if he could."

"I'm happy I can be here," Lou said graciously. "But before we get into that story, Bud, I think you should hear about Tom's experience last night."

"Oh, yes, Tom, I'm sorry. Tell me about your evening."

I don't know why, perhaps because I worked for Bud and wanted badly to impress him, but I was reticent at first to share what I had shared with Lou. But Lou kept prodding me—'Tell him about this' and 'Tell him about that'—and I soon relaxed and told Bud all about my evening. After 10 minutes or so, he was smiling, just as Lou had been.

"That's terrific, Tom," Bud said. "How was Todd through the evening?"

"About the same as usual—pretty silent. He basically responded to my questions as he always does—mostly with 'Yes,' 'No,' and 'I don't know.' But I didn't seem to mind it last night, whereas before it would've driven me crazy."

"That reminds me of *my* boy," Lou said. He paused for a moment, looking out the window, far away, as if retrieving something from the distant past. "The story of Zagrum's turn-around starts with him."

18   *Leadership in the Box*

"My youngest boy, Cory, who's now almost 40, was a handful. Drugs, drinking—you name it, he did it. Everything came to a head when he was arrested for selling drugs during his senior year in high school.

"At first I wanted to deny it. No Herbert ever did drugs. And to sell them—that was unthinkable. I stomped around demanding that this injustice be exposed. It couldn't be true. Not about *my* boy. So I demanded a full trial. Our lawyer recommended against it, and the district attorney offered a plea bargain that included only 30 days in jail. But I wouldn't have it. 'I'll be damned if my son is ever going to go to jail,' I said. And so we fought.

"But we lost, and Cory ended up spending a full year in the youth detention facility up in Bridgeport. As far as I was concerned, it was a blight on the family name. I visited him twice the whole year.

"When he got home, we hardly spoke. I rarely asked him anything, and when I did, he responded with barely audible one-word answers. He fell back into the wrong crowd, and within three months he was arrested again, for shoplifting.

"I wanted to deal with this one quietly. I had no illusions that he was innocent, so I pushed for a plea bargain that involved a 60-day wilderness treatment and survival program in the high country of Arizona. Five days later, I boarded a plane, Cory in tow, from JFK to Phoenix. I was taking him to be 'fixed.'

"My wife, Carol, and I dropped him off at the organization's headquarters. We watched as he was loaded into a van with other kids who were entering the program, and away they drove toward the mountains of eastern central Arizona. We were then escorted into a room for two all-day sessions — sessions where I expected to learn how the people there were going to fix my son.

"But that's not what I learned. I learned that whatever my son's problems might be, *I* needed fixing, too. What I learned changed my life. Not at first, for I fought everything they were suggesting tooth and nail: 'What, *me?*' I protested. '*I* don't do drugs. *I'm* not the one who spent most of my senior year in high school behind bars. *I'm* not the thief. I'm a responsible person — respected, the president of a company, even.' But gradually I came to see the lie in my defensiveness. I came to discover, in a way I can describe only as simultaneously painful and hopeful, that I had been, for years, in the box toward my wife and my kids."

"In the box?" I said quietly, almost under my breath.

"Yes. In the box," Lou responded. "I learned that first day in Arizona what you learned yesterday. And in that moment — about the time when my son was probably climbing out of the van and looking around at the isolated wilderness that would be his home for the next two months — I felt for the first time in years an overwhelming desire to take him in my arms and hold him. What desperate loneliness and shame he must have been feeling. And how I had added to it! His last hours — or, for that matter, months and maybe even years — with his dad had been spent under a silent cloud of blame. It was all I could do to hold back the tears.

"But it was worse than that. That day, I realized that my box had driven away not only my son but also the most important people in my company. Two weeks earlier, in what people around the company were calling the 'March Meltdown,' five of the six executive team members had left for 'better opportunities.'"

"Kate?" I asked.

"Yes. Kate was one of them."

Lou stared intently into nowhere, apparently in deep thought. "It's amazing when I think back on it now," he said finally. "I felt betrayed by them the same way I felt betrayed by Cory. *To hell with them*, I told myself. *To hell with them all.*

"I was determined," he continued, "to build Zagrum into a success without them. *They weren't that great anyway*, I told myself. They'd been around, most of them, for the full six or so years since I'd purchased the company from John Zagrum, and the company was basically limping along. *If they were any good, we'd be doing better by now*, I thought. *To hell with them.*

"But it was a lie. Now it might have been true that we should've been doing better. But it was still a lie—because I was completely blind to my own role in our mediocrity. And as a result, I was blind to how I was blaming them *not* for *their* mistakes, but for *mine*. I was blind, as we always are, to my own box.

"But I recovered my sight in Arizona. I saw in myself a leader who was so sure of the brilliance of his own ideas that he couldn't allow brilliance in anyone else's, a leader who felt he was so 'enlightened' that he needed to see workers negatively in order to prove his enlightenment, a leader so driven to be the best that he made sure no one else could be as good as he was."

Lou paused. "You've learned about collusion, haven't you, Tom?"

"Where two or more people are mutually in their boxes toward each other? Yes."

"Well, with self-justifying images that told me I was brilliant, enlightened, and the best, you can imagine the collusions I was provoking around here. In the box, I was a walking excuse factory—both for myself and for others. Any workers who needed the slightest justification for their own self-betrayals had a smorgasbord of options in me.

"I couldn't see, for example, that the more I took responsibility for my team's performance, the more mistrusted they felt. They then resisted in all kinds of ways: Some just gave up and left all creativity to me, others defied me and did things their own way, and still others left the company altogether. All of these responses convinced me all the more of the incompetence of the people in the company, so I responded by issuing even more careful instructions, developing even more policies and procedures, and so on. Everyone took all that to be further evidence of my disrespect for them and resisted me all the more. And so on, round and round—each of us inviting the other to be in the box, and in so doing, providing each other with mutual justification for *staying there*. Collusion was everywhere. We were a mess."

"Just like Semmelweis," I said in amazement, under my breath.

"Oh, so Bud told you about Semmelweis?" Lou asked, looking at Bud and then back at me.

"Yes," I said, nodding along with Bud.

"Well, that's right," Lou continued. "The Semmelweis story is an interesting parallel. I was, in effect, killing the people in my company. Our turnover rate rivaled the mortality rate at Vienna General. I was carrying the disease I blamed everyone else for. I infected them and then blamed them for the infection. Our organizational chart was a chart of colluding boxes. As I said, we were a mess.

"But what I learned in Arizona was that *I* was a mess. Because I was in the box, I was provoking the very problems I was complaining about. I had chased away the very best people I knew—feeling justified all the time, because in my box, I was convinced they weren't that good."

He paused. "Even Kate," he added, shaking his head. "No one on this planet is any more talented than Kate, but I couldn't see that because of my box.

"So as I sat there in Arizona, I had a huge problem. I was sitting next to a wife whom I'd been taking for granted for 25 years. I was by then 100 miles of impassable terrain away from a son whose only recent memories of his father were probably bitter ones. And my company had come unglued— the best and brightest scattering around the globe, embarking on new careers. I was a lonely man. My box was destroying everything I cared about.

"One question seemed more important to me in that moment than anything else in the world: *How can I possibly get out of the box?*"

Lou paused, and I waited for him to continue.

"So how *do* you?" I finally interjected. "How *do* you get out of the box?"

"You already know."

19 *Toward Being out of the Box*

"I do?" I searched my memory about the session the day before. I was sure we hadn't talked about it.

"Yes. And so did I when I was wondering how to get out," Lou said.

"Huh?" At that moment I was really lost.

"Think about it," Lou replied. "As I sat there regretting how I'd acted toward my wife, my son, and my coworkers, what were they to me? In that moment, was I seeing them as people or as objects?"

"In that moment, they were people to you," I said, my voice trailing off in thought.

"Yes. My blame, resentment, and indifference were gone. I was seeing them as they were, and I was regretting having treated them as *less* than that. So in that moment, where was I?"

"You were out of the box," I said softly, almost as if in a trance, trying to locate what made the change possible. I was feeling a bit like a spectator at a magic show who sees the rabbit surely enough but has no idea where it came from.

"Exactly," Lou agreed. "In the moment I felt the keen desire to be out of the box for them, I was *already* out of the box toward them. To feel that desire for them *was* to be out of the box toward them.

"And the same goes for you, Tom," he continued. "Think about your time last night with your family. What were they to you last night? Were you seeing them as people or as objects?"

"They were people," I said, amazed by the discovery.

"So if last night you were out of the box," Lou said, "then you already know how to get out of the box."

"But I don't," I said in protest. "I have no idea how it happened. In fact, I didn't even know I was out of the box last night until you just pointed it out to me. I couldn't begin to tell you how I got out."

"Yes you can. In fact, you already did."

"What do you mean?" I was completely bewildered.

"I mean, you told us about yesterday and about your experience last night, about how you went home and spent the evening with your family. That story teaches us how to get out of the box."

"But that's my point. I don't see it."

"And this is my point: Yes you do. You just don't realize it yet. But you will."

That gave me a little bit of comfort, but not much.

"You see," Lou said, "the question 'How do I get out of the box?' is really two questions. The first question is 'How do I *get* out?' and the second is 'How do I *stay* out once I'm out?' The question you're really worried about, I think, is the second—how you stay out. Think about it, and I want to emphasize this again: When you're feeling that you want to be out of the box for someone, in that moment you're already out. You're feeling that way *because* you're now seeing him or her as a person. In feeling that way toward that person, you're *already* out of the box. So in that moment—like the moment you're having right now and like last night—when you're seeing and feeling clearly and want to be out of the box for others, what you're really asking is this: 'What can I do to *stay* out of the box toward them? What can I do to sustain the change I'm now feeling?' That's the question. And there are some pretty specific things we can do, once we're out of the box, to *stay* out of the box—and particularly for our purposes, in the workplace."

As Lou was talking, I started to understand what he meant. "Okay. I see how in feeling like I want to be out of the box for someone, in that moment I'm seeing him or her as a person, so in having that feeling, I'm already out of the box toward that person. I understand that. And I understand how once I am out of the box, the question then is how to stay out—and I definitely want to get into that. Especially applied to work. But I'm still scratching my head over how I got out in the first place—how my resentment toward Laura and Todd suddenly disappeared. Maybe I just got lucky last night. When I'm not so lucky, I'd like to know how to get myself out."

"Fair enough," Lou said, standing up. "I'll do my best, with Bud's help, to explain how we get out in the first place."

20   *Dead Ends*

"To begin with," Lou continued, "it helps to understand how we *don't* get out of the box."

He wrote on the board, "What doesn't work in the box." Turning back to me, he said, "Think about the things we try to do when we're in the box. For example, in the box, whom do we think has the problem?"

"Others," I answered.

"That's right," he said, "so normally we spend a lot of energy in the box trying to change others. But does that work? Does that get us out of the box?"

"No."

"Why not?" he asked.

"Because that's the problem in the first place," I said. "I'm trying to change them because, in the box, I think they need to be changed."

"But does that mean no one needs to be changed?" Lou asked. "Is everyone doing things just perfectly, then? Is that what you're saying—that no one needs to *improve?*"

I felt a little stupid when he asked the question. *Come on, Callum,* I said to myself. *Think!* I wasn't being careful enough. "No, of course not. Everyone needs to improve."

"Then why not the *other* guy?" he said. "What's wrong if I want *him* to improve?"

That was a good question. *What is wrong with that?* I asked myself. I thought that was what all this meant, but at that moment I wasn't so certain. "I'm not sure," I said.

"Well, think about it this way. While it's true that others may have problems they need to solve, are *their* problems the reason I'm in the box?"

"No. That's what you think in the box, but it's a misperception."

"Exactly," said Lou. "So even if I were successful and the person I tried to change actually changed, would that solve the problem of my being in the box?"

"No, I guess it wouldn't."

"That's right, it wouldn't—even if the other person actually *did* change."

"And it's worse than that," Bud interjected. "Think about what we talked about yesterday regarding collusion: When I'm in the box and try to get others to change, do I invite them to change as I'd like?"

"No," I said. "You end up provoking just the opposite."

"Exactly right," Bud said. "My box ends up provoking more of the very thing I set out to change. So if I try to get out by changing others, I end up provoking others to give me reason to *stay* in the box."

"So," Lou said, turning to the board and writing, "trying to change others doesn't work."

WHAT DOESN'T WORK IN THE BOX

1. Trying to change others

"What about doing my best to *cope* with others?" Lou said, turning from the board. "Does that work?"

"I wouldn't think so," I said. "That's essentially what I usually do. But it doesn't seem to get me out."

"That's right, it doesn't," Lou agreed. "And there's a simple reason why. 'Coping' has the same deficiency as trying to change the other person: It's just another way to continue blaming. It communicates the blame of my box, which invites those I'm coping with to be in *their* boxes."

He turned to the board and added "coping" to the list of things that didn't work.

WHAT DOESN'T WORK IN THE BOX

1. Trying to change others

2. Doing my best to "cope" with others

"How about this one?" Bud added while Lou was writing. "Leaving. Does leaving work? Will that get me out of the box?"

"Maybe," I said. "It seems like it might sometimes."

"Well, let's think about it. Where do I think the problem is when I'm in the box?"

"In others," I said.

"Exactly. But where *in fact* is the problem when I'm in the box?"

"In myself."

"Yes. So if I leave, what goes with me?" he asked.

"The problem," I said softly, nodding. "I get it. The box goes with me."

"That's right," Bud said. "In the box, leaving is just another way to blame. It's just a continuation of my box. I take my self-justifying feelings with me. Now it may be that in certain situations, leaving is the right thing to do. But leaving a situation will never be sufficient, even if right. Ultimately, I have to leave my box too."

135

"Yeah, that makes sense," I said.

"Here, let me add that to the list," Lou said.

WHAT DOESN'T WORK IN THE BOX

1. Trying to change others

2. Doing my best to "cope" with others

3. Leaving

"Here's another one to consider," said Lou. "How about communicating? Will that work? Will that get me out of the box?"

"It *seems* like it would," I said. "I mean, if you can't communicate, you don't have anything."

"Okay," said Lou, "let's consider this one carefully." He looked at the board. "Whose story is this over here about self-betrayal—is it yours, Bud?"

"Yes," Bud nodded.

"Oh yes, I see Nancy's name there," said Lou. "Okay, let's think about it. Look here, Tom, at Bud's story. After he betrayed himself, here's how he saw Nancy—as lazy, inconsiderate, insensitive, and so on. Now here's the question. If he tries to communicate with Nancy now, while he's in his box, what's he going to communicate?"

"Oh," I said, surprised by the implication. "He's going to communicate what he's feeling about her—namely, that she's all of those bad things."

"Exactly. And will that help? Is Bud likely to get out of the box by telling his wife that she's all the lousy things he's thinking she is when he's in the box?"

"No," I said. "But what if he's a little more sophisticated than that? I mean, with a little skill, he might be able to communicate more subtly and not just come right out and blast away."

"That's true," Lou agreed. "But remember, if Bud's in the box, then he's blaming. It's true he may be able to acquire some skills that would improve his communication techniques, but do you suppose those skills would hide his blame?"

"Probably not," I said. "At least not completely."

"That's the way it seems to me too," agreed Lou. "In the box, whether I'm a skilled communicator or not, I end up communicating my box—and that's the problem."

He turned and added "communicating" to the list.

WHAT DOESN'T WORK IN THE BOX

1. Trying to change others

2. Doing my best to "cope" with others

3. Leaving

4. Communicating

"In fact," he said, backing away from the board, "this point about skills applies to skills generally, not just to communication skills. You might think about it this way: No matter what skill you teach me, I can be either *in* the box or *out of* the box when I implement it. And that raises this question: Will using a skill *in* the box be the way to get *out of* the box?"

"No," I said, "I guess not."

"That's why skill training in nontechnical areas often has so little lasting impact," Lou said. "Helpful skills and techniques aren't very helpful if they're done in the box. They just provide people with more-sophisticated ways to blame."

"And remember, Tom," added Bud, "the people problems that most people try to correct with skills aren't due to a lack of skill at all. They're due to self-betrayal. People problems seem intractable not because they are insoluble but because the common skill interventions are not themselves solutions."

"That's exactly right," agreed Lou. "So," he said, turning and writing again, "we can't get out of the box simply by implementing new skills and techniques."

WHAT DOESN'T WORK IN THE BOX

1. Trying to change others

2. Doing my best to "cope" with others

3. Leaving

4. Communicating

5. Implementing new skills or techniques

I looked at the board and suddenly felt depressed. *What is left?* I thought.

"There's one more possibility we should consider," said Bud. "Here it is: What if I try to change *myself—my behavior?* Can that get me out of the box?"

"It looks like that's the only thing that *can* get you out," I answered.

"This is tricky, but quite important." Bud stood up and started to pace. "Let's think back to a couple of the stories we talked about yesterday. . . . Remember the situation I told you about Gabe and Leon over in Building 6?"

I searched my memory. "I'm not sure."

"Gabe had tried doing all kinds of things to let Leon know he was concerned about him."

"Oh yeah, I remember."

"Well," he continued, "Gabe had changed his behavior toward Leon dramatically. But did that work?"

"No."

"And why not?"

"Because, as I recall, Gabe didn't really care about Leon, and that's what Leon understood despite all of Gabe's outward changes."

"Exactly. Since Gabe was in the box toward Leon, every new thing Gabe tried to do from within his box just amounted to a change within the box. Leon remained an object to him throughout all his efforts.

"Think about that," Bud said with emphasis. "Or think about the story where Nancy and I were arguing but I tried to apologize and put an end to it. Do you remember?"

I nodded, "Yeah."

"It's the same thing," he said, taking his seat. "I changed myself in a radical way in that case: I changed all the way from arguing to kissing. But did that change get me out of the box?"

"No, because you didn't really mean it," I answered. "You were still *in* the box."

"And that's just the point," Bud said, leaning toward me. "Because I was in the box, I *couldn't* mean it. In the box, every change I can think of is just a change in my style of being in the box. I can change from arguing to kissing. I can change from ignoring someone to going out of my way to shower that person with attention. But whatever changes I think of in the box are changes I think of from *within* the box, and they are therefore just more *of* the box—which is the problem in the first place. Others remain objects to me."

"That's right," Lou said, moving to the board. "So consider the implication, Tom. I can't get out of the box merely by changing my behavior."

WHAT DOESN'T WORK IN THE BOX

1. Trying to change others

2. Doing my best to "cope" with others

3. Leaving

4. Communicating

5. Implementing new skills or techniques

6. Changing my behavior

"But wait a minute," I said. "You're telling me that I can't get out by trying to change others or by doing my best to cope with others or by leaving, communicating, or implementing new skills and techniques. And then you're telling me on top of that that I can't even get out of the box by changing *myself*?"

"Well, you can't get out by continuing to *focus on yourself*—which is what you do when you try to change your behavior in the box. So yes, that *is* what we're saying," he answered calmly.

"Then how could we *ever* get out? I mean, if what you're saying is right, then there's no way out. We're all stuck."

"Actually," Lou said, "that's not quite right. There *is* a way out, but it's different than anyone generally supposes. And you know what it is, just like I told you before. You just don't realize that you know it."

I was listening intently. I wanted to understand this.

"You were out of the box last night toward your family, right?"

"I guess so."

"Well, by the way you told your story, it sounded like you were," Lou said. "That means there *is* a way out. So let's think of your experience last night. Did you try to change your wife and son last night?"

"No."

"Did you feel like you were 'coping' with them?"

"No."

"And obviously you didn't leave. How about communicating? Did you get out because you communicated?"

"Well, maybe. I mean, we communicated very well — the best we'd done in a long time."

"Yes," Lou agreed, "but did you get out of the box because you communicated, or did you communicate well because you were out of the box?"

"Let me think," I said, more puzzled than ever. "I was already out of the box — I was out of the box on my way home. Communicating isn't what *got* me out, I guess."

"Okay, then how about this last one?" Lou said, pointing at the list. "Did you get out of the box because you focused on and tried to change *yourself?*"

I sat there wondering, *What happened to me yesterday?* It ended in a magnificent evening, but I suddenly had no idea how I had gotten there. It was like I'd been abducted by aliens. *Did I set out to change myself?* That wasn't my memory. It felt more like something changed me. At least, I couldn't remember setting out to change. In fact, if anything, it seemed that along the whole way, I *resisted* the suggestion that I had to change. *So what happened? How did I get out of the box? Why did my feelings change?*

"I'm not sure," I said finally. "But I don't remember trying to change myself. Somehow, I just ended up changed — almost like something changed me. But I'm clueless as to how it happened."

"Here's something that might help you figure it out," Bud said. "Remember when we talked yesterday about how the distinction between being in the box and being out of the box is deeper than behavior?"

"Yeah, I remember that," I said.

"And we discussed the airplane-seating story, drew that diagram with behaviors up on top, and talked about how we can do almost any behavior in one of those two ways—either out of the box or in the box. Remember?"

"Yes."

"So consider this: If being in or out of the box is something that's deeper than behavior, do you suppose the key to getting out of the box will be a behavior?"

I started to see what he was saying. "No, I guess it wouldn't," I said, suddenly feeling hopeful that this thought would lead me to the answer.

"That's right," Bud said. "One of the reasons you may be struggling to understand how you got out of the box is that you're trying to identify a *behavior* that got you out. But since the box itself is deeper than behavior, the way out of the box has to be deeper than behavior, too. Almost any behavior can be done either in the box or out of the box, so no mere behavior can get you out. You're looking in the wrong place."

"In other words," Lou interjected, "there's a fundamental problem with the question, 'What do I need to *do* to get out of the box?' The problem is that anything I tell you to do can be done either *in* or *out of* the box. And if done in the box, that 'in-the-box' behavior can't be the way to get out. So you might then be tempted to say, 'Well, the answer, then, is to do that behavior out of the box.' Fair enough. But if you're out of the box, then you won't need the behavior anymore to *get* you out. Either way, the behavior isn't what gets you out. It's something else."

"But *what?*" I pleaded.

"Something right in front of you."

21 *The Way Out*

"Think about yesterday," Lou continued. "You just said that it felt like something changed you. We need to think about that a little more carefully."

He moved toward the board. "I want to talk about self-betrayal and the box for a moment—to make something clear that may not have been made explicit yet." He drew the following diagram:

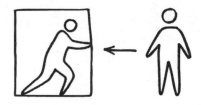

"To begin with, here's a picture of what life is like in the box," he said, pointing at his drawing. "The box is a metaphor for how I'm *resisting* others. By 'resisting,' I mean that my self-betrayal isn't passive. In the box, I'm actively resisting what the humanity of others calls me to do for them.

"For example," he said, pointing to Bud's story on the board, "in the story here about Bud's failing to get up so that Nancy could sleep, that initial feeling was an impression he had of something he should do for Nancy. He betrayed himself when he *resisted* that sense of what he should do for her, and in resisting that sense, he began to focus on himself and to see her as being undeserving of help. His self-deception—his 'box'—is something he created and sustained through his active resistance of Nancy. This is why it's futile, as Bud was saying a few minutes ago, to try to get out of the box by focusing further on ourselves: In the box, everything we think and feel is part of the lie of the box. The truth is, we change in the moment we cease resisting what is *outside* our box—others. Does that make sense?"

"Yeah, I think so."

"In the moment we cease resisting others, we're out of the box—liberated from self-justifying thoughts and feelings. This is why the way out of the box is always right before our eyes— *because the people we're resisting are right before our eyes.* We can stop betraying ourselves toward them—we can stop *resisting* the call of their humanity upon us."

"But what can help me to do *that?*" I asked.

Lou looked at me thoughtfully. "There's something else you should understand about self-betrayal—something that may give you the leverage you're looking for. Think about your experience yesterday with Bud and Kate. How would you characterize it? Would you say that you were basically *in* or *out of* the box toward them?"

"Oh, *out,* for sure," I said. "At least most of the time," I added, giving Bud a sheepish grin. He smiled in return.

"But you've also indicated that you were *in* the box toward Laura yesterday. So there is a sense in which you were both in *and* out of the box at the same time—in the box toward Laura but out of the box toward Bud and Kate."

"Yeah, I guess that's right."

"This is an important point, Tom. Toward any one person or group of people, I'm either in or out of the box at any given moment. But since there are many people in my life— some that I may be more in the box toward than others—in an important sense, I can be both in *and* out of the box at the same time. In the box toward some people and out toward others.

"This simple fact can give us leverage to get out of the box in the areas of our lives where we may be struggling. In fact, that's what happened to you yesterday. Let me show you what I mean."

Lou walked to the board and modified his drawing.

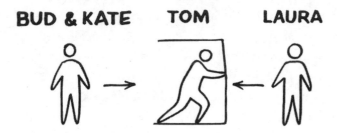

BUD & KATE   TOM   LAURA

"Here's how we might depict what you were like yesterday," he said, standing to the side of the board. "You were in the box toward Laura but out of the box as you engaged with Bud and Kate. Now notice: Although you were resistant to Laura's needs because you were in the box toward her, you nevertheless retained a sense of what people generally might need because you were out of the box toward others— namely, Bud and Kate. This sense that you felt and honored regarding Bud and Kate, combined with the continual call of Laura's humanity to you—which is always there—is what made getting out of the box toward Laura possible.

"So although it's true that there is nothing we can think of and do from within the box to get ourselves out, the fact that we are almost always both in and out of the box at the same time, albeit in different directions, means that we always have it within our capacity to find our way to a perspective within ourselves that is out of the box. This is what Bud and Kate did for you yesterday—they supplied for you an out-of-the box environment from which you were able to consider your in-the-box relationships with new clarity. From the context of your relationships with Bud and Kate, you were able to think of a number of things you could do to help reduce your in-the-box moments and heal your in-the-box relationships. In fact, there is one thing in particular that you did while you were out of the box toward Bud and Kate that helped you to get out of the box toward Laura."

My mind searched for the answer. "What did I do?"

"You questioned your own virtue."

"I what?"

"You questioned your own virtue. While you were *out of* the box, you listened to what Bud and Kate taught you about being *in* the box. And then you applied it to your own personal situations. The out-of-the-box nature of your experience with Bud and Kate invited you to do something that we never do in the box—it invited you to question whether you were in fact as out of the box as you had assumed you were in other areas of your life. And what you learned from the vantage point of that out-of-the-box space transformed your view of Laura.

"Now that probably didn't happen right off the bat," he continued, "but I'd bet there was a moment when it was as if the light came pouring in—a moment when your blaming emotions toward Laura seemed to evaporate, and she suddenly seemed different to you than she had the moment before."

That was exactly how it happened, I thought to myself. I remembered that moment—when I saw the hypocrisy in my anger. It was as if everything changed in an instant. "That's true," I said. "That's what happened."

"Then we need to modify this drawing still more," Lou said, turning to the board. When he finished, he backed away from the board and said, "This is how you looked when you left last night."

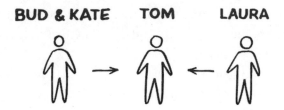

BUD & KATE   TOM   LAURA

"You were seeing and feeling straightforwardly. Laura seemed different to you because in the moment you got out of the box toward her, you no longer had the need to blame her and inflate her faults."

Lou sat down. "In a way," he said, "this is quite a miraculous thing. But in another way, it's the most common thing in the world. It happens all the time in our lives—usually on very small matters that are quickly forgotten. All of us are both in the box and out of the box toward others. The more we can find our way to the out-of-the-box vantage points within us, the more readily we will be able to shine light on the in-the-box justifications we are carrying. All of a sudden, because of the presence of the people who continually stand before us, *and* because of what we know as we stand out of the box in relation to other people, our box can be penetrated by the humanity of those whom we've been resisting. When that happens, we know in that moment what we need to do: We need to honor them as *people*. And in that moment—the moment I see another as a person, with needs, hopes, and worries as real and legitimate as my own—I am out of the box toward him. What remains for me, then, is the question of whether I am going to *stay* out."

"You might think about it this way," Bud interjected. "Look again at this story," he said, pointing to the diagram of his crying-baby story. "When I once again have a feeling of something I desire to do to help another, where am I in this diagram?"

I looked at the board. "You're at the top again—back at the feeling."

"Exactly. I'm back out of the box. I can now choose the other way. I can now choose to honor that sense rather than betray it. And that, Tom—acting on the sense or feeling I have recovered of what I can do to help another—is the key to *staying* out of the box. Having recovered that sense, I am out of the box; by choosing to honor it rather than betray it, I am choosing to stay out of the box."

"In fact, Tom," Lou added, "I bet you had a feeling as you left here yesterday that there were some things you needed to do for some people last night. Am I right?"

"Yes," I said.

"And you did them, didn't you?" Lou asked.

"Yes, I did."

"That's why your night went as it did," he said. "You got out of the box toward Laura, and Todd for that matter, during your time with Bud and Kate. But your night went well because you *stayed* out of the box by doing for your family what you felt you should do."

What Lou said seemed to explain my night with Laura and Todd well enough, but it left me feeling a little confused and overwhelmed about situations in general. How could people be expected to do everything they felt they should do for others? That didn't seem right.

"Are you saying that in order to stay out of the box, I have to always be doing things for others?"

Lou smiled. "That's an important question. We need to consider it with some care—maybe with a specific example." He paused for a moment. "Let's think about driving. What would you say is your standard attitude toward other drivers on the road?"

I smiled to myself as I recalled a number of characteristic commutes. I remembered waving my fist at a driver who wouldn't slow down to let me merge, only to discover, after I'd forced my way in, that he was my neighbor. And I remembered glaring at the driver of a maddeningly slow car as I sped around him, only to discover, to my horror, that he was the same neighbor. "I suppose I'm pretty indifferent toward them," I chuckled, unable to suppress my amusement. "Unless, of course, they're in my way."

"It sounds like we went to the same driving school," Lou quipped. "But you know what? Occasionally I've had very different feelings toward other drivers. For example, it sometimes occurs to me that each of these people on the road is just as busy as I am and just as wrapped up in his or her own life as I am in mine. And in these moments, when I get out of the box toward them, other drivers seem very different to me. In a way, I feel that I understand them and can relate to them, even though I know basically nothing about them."

"Yeah," I nodded, "I've had that experience, too."

"Good. So you know what I'm talking about. With that kind of experience in mind, let's consider your question.

You're worried that in order to stay out of the box, you have to do everything that pops into your head to do for others. And that seems overwhelming, if not foolhardy. Am I right?"

"Yes. That's one way to put it."

"Well," said Lou, "we need to consider whether being out of the box creates the overwhelming stream of obligations you're worried about. Let's consider the driving situation. First of all, think of the people in the cars far ahead and far behind me. Is my being out of the box likely to make much of a difference in my outward behavior toward *them?*"

"No, I suppose not."

"How about toward drivers who are nearer to me? Would my being out of the box change my outward behavior toward *them?*"

"Probably."

"Okay, how? What might I do differently?"

I thought of seeing my neighbor in my rearview mirror. "You probably wouldn't cut people off as much."

"Good. What else?"

"You'd probably drive more safely, more considerately. And who knows?" I added, thinking of the glare I shot at the man who turned out to be my neighbor, "you might even smile more."

"All right, good enough. Now notice—do these behavioral changes strike you as overwhelming or burdensome?"

"Well, no."

"So, in this case, being out of the box and seeing others as people doesn't mean that I'm suddenly bombarded with burdensome obligations. It simply means that I'm seeing and appreciating others as people while I'm driving, or shopping, or doing whatever it is I am doing.

"In other cases," he continued, "getting out of the box may mean that I relinquish a prejudice that I have held toward those not like myself—people of a different race, for example, or faith, or culture. I will be less judgmental when I see them as people than when I saw them as objects. I will treat them with more courtesy and respect. Again, however, do such changes seem burdensome to you?"

I shook my head. "On the contrary, they seem freeing."

"That's the way it seems to me too," Lou said. "But let me add one more point." He leaned forward and folded his arms on the table. "On occasion, there *are* times when we have specific impressions of additional things we should do for others, particularly toward people we spend more time with—family members, for example, or friends or work associates. We know these people; we have a pretty good sense of their hopes, needs, cares, and fears; and we're more likely to have wronged them. All of this increases the obligation we feel toward them, as well it should.

"Now, as we've been talking about, in order to stay out of the box, it's critical that we honor what our out-of-the-box sensibility tells us we should do for these people. However—and this is important—this doesn't necessarily mean that we end up doing everything we feel would be ideal. For we have our *own* responsibilities and needs that require attention, and it may be that we can't help others as much or as soon as we wish we could. In such cases, we will have no need to blame them and justify ourselves because we will still be seeing them as people that we want to help even if we are unable to help at that very moment or in the way we think would be ideal. We simply do the best we can under the circumstances.

It may not be the ideal, but it will be the best we can do—offered because we *want* to do it."

Lou looked at me steadily. "You've learned about self-justifying images, haven't you?"

"Yes."

"Then you understand how we live insecurely when we're in the box, desperate to show that we're justified—that we're thoughtful, for example, or worthy or noble. It can feel pretty overwhelming always having to demonstrate our virtue. In fact, when we're feeling overwhelmed, it generally isn't our obligation to others but our in-the-box desperation to prove something about *ourselves* that we find overwhelming. If you look back on your life, I think you'll find that that's the case—you've probably felt overwhelmed, overobligated, and overburdened far more often *in* the box than *out*. To begin with, you might compare your night last night with the nights that came before."

That's true, I thought. *Last night—the first time in a while that I'd actually gone out of my way to do something for Laura and Todd—was the easiest night I'd had in I don't know how long.*

Lou paused for a few moments, and Bud asked, "Does that help with your question, Tom?"

"Yeah. It helps a lot." Then I smiled at Lou. "Thanks."

Lou nodded at me and settled back in his chair, apparently satisfied. He looked past me, out the window. Bud and I waited for him to speak.

"As I sat there those many years ago in that seminar room in Arizona," he said finally, "learning from others just as you've learned here from Bud and Kate, my boxes started to melt away. I felt deep regret at how I'd acted toward the people in my company. And in the moment I felt that regret, I was out of the box toward them.

"The future of Zagrum depended," he continued, "on whether I could *stay* out of the box. But I knew that in order to stay out, there were certain things I had to do. And fast."

"In order to see what I needed to do," Lou said, rising from his chair, "you need to understand what the nature of my self-betrayal was." He began to pace the length of the table. "There were many self-betrayals, I suppose, but I realized as I pondered the implications of what I learned in Arizona that I'd betrayed myself at work in one major way. And what we've discovered in the years since is that almost everyone at work betrays himself or herself in this same foundational way. So everything we do here is designed to help our people avoid that self-betrayal and stay out of the box. Our success in *that* endeavor has been the key to our success in the marketplace."

"So what is it?" I asked.

"Well, let me ask you this," Lou said. "What's the purpose of our efforts at work?"

"To achieve results together," I answered.

Lou stopped. "Excellent," he said, apparently impressed.

"Actually, Bud talked about that yesterday," I said, slightly sheepish.

"Oh, did you already talk about the foundational workplace self-betrayal?" he asked, looking at Bud.

"No. We touched on how in the box we can't truly focus on results because we're so busy focusing on ourselves," Bud said, "but we didn't get specific about it."

"Okay," Lou responded. "Well then, Tom, you've been with us now for what—a month or so?"

"Yes."

"Tell me about how you came to join Zagrum."

I related to Lou and Bud my career highlights at Tetrix, my longtime admiration of Zagrum, and the details of my interviewing process.

"Tell me how you felt when you were offered the job."

"Oh, I was ecstatic."

"The day before you started, did you have good feelings about your soon-to-be coworkers?" Lou asked.

"Sure," I answered. "I was excited to get started."

"Did you feel that you wanted to be helpful to them?"

"Yes, absolutely."

"And as you thought about what you would do at Zagrum and how you would *be* on the job, what was your vision?"

"Well, I saw myself working hard and doing the best I could to help Zagrum succeed," I answered.

"Okay," Lou said, "so what you're saying is that before you started, you had a sense that you should do your best to help Zagrum and the people who are part of it succeed—or, as you said earlier, achieve results."

"Yes," I answered.

Lou walked over to the board. "Is it okay with you, Bud," he said, pointing toward the diagram of Bud's crying-baby story, "if I change this a little?"

"Absolutely. Please go ahead," Bud said.

Lou edited the diagram and then turned to face me.

"Notice, Tom," he said, "that when most people start a job, their feelings are similar to yours. They're grateful for the employment and for the opportunity. They want to do their best—for their company and for the people in it.

"But interview those same people a year later," he said, "and their feelings are usually very different. Their feelings

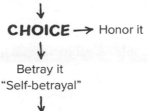

SENSE
Do my best to help the company and the
people within it achieve results

⬇

CHOICE ➜ Honor it

⬇

Betray it
"Self-betrayal"

⬇

HOW I STARTED TO SEE **MYSELF**	HOW I STARTED TO SEE **COWORKERS**	
• Victim	• Lazy	Lack of commitment
• Hardworking	• Inconsiderate	Lack of engagement
• Important	• Unappreciative	Troublemaking
• Fair	• Insensitive	Conflict
• Sensitive	• Fakers	Lack of motivation
• Good manager	• Lousy managers	Stress
• Good worker	• Lousy workers	Poor teamwork
		Backbiting/bad attitudes
		Misalignment
		Lack of trust
		Lack of accountability
		Communication problems

toward many of their coworkers frequently resemble the feelings Bud had toward Nancy in the story he told. And you'll often find that people who formerly were committed, engaged, motivated, looking forward to working as a team, and so on, now have problems in many of those areas. And who do you suppose they think *caused* those problems?"

"Everyone else in the company," I answered. "The boss, coworkers, the people who report to them—even the company, for that matter."

"Yes. But now we know better," he said. "When we blame, we blame because of ourselves, not because of others."

"But is that always the case?" I asked. "I mean, when I was at Tetrix, my boss was terrible. He created all kinds of trouble. And now I see why—he was deep in the box. He mistreated everyone in the division."

"Yes," Lou said, "and as hard as we work at this at Zagrum, you're going to run into people who mistreat you here as well. But look at this diagram," he said, pointing at the board. "Is this worker blaming his coworkers because of what they've done to him, whatever that might be? Or another way to put it is this: Do we get in the box because other people are in *their* boxes? Is that what causes us to get in the box?"

"No," I said, "we get in the box through our own self-betrayals. I understand that. But I guess my question is, isn't it possible to blame someone without being in the box?"

Lou looked at me intently. "Do you have a specific example that we could consider?"

"Sure," I said, "I'm still thinking about my old boss at Tetrix. I guess I've been blaming him for a long time. But my point is, he really *is* a jerk. He's a big problem."

Lou sat down. "Let's think about that," he said. "Do you suppose it's possible to recognize how someone might be a big problem without being in the box and blaming him?"

"Yeah, I guess so," I answered.

"Do you suppose I can even assign responsibility for something to someone—because a particular person really did cause a problem, for example?" Lou asked.

"It seems like you could, but it also seems like you and Bud and Kate have been saying that that's something that can't be done out of the box."

"Then we've been unclear," Lou replied. "Being out of the box actually allows a person to be able to assign or assess responsibility with clarity, and the reason for that is because his vision is not clouded by the box. He is not, for example, assigning responsibility to another in order to escape responsibility himself. Because he isn't, his act of assigning responsibility does not feel personal or offensive. In fact, assigning responsibility in such a case is actually a way of helping someone. It is an entirely different thing, however, to excuse one's own role in a problem through the guise of holding another responsible. It is this latter act that we call 'blame,' and blaming is precisely what we do instead of objectively assessing levels of responsibility whenever we are in the box. We blame others not to help them but to help ourselves.

"Which brings us back to your question, Tom. In your prior job, when you were thinking that your old boss was a real jerk, were you trying to help him, or was this judgment of him really a way of just helping yourself?"

I suddenly felt entirely exposed, as if a lie were about to become public knowledge.

"Another way to ask that," Lou continued, "would be to ask whether your blame-filled efforts with your old boss helped him to get any better."

"Probably not," I murmured.

"Probably?" Lou asked.

I didn't know what to say. The truth was, there *was* no out-of-the-box purpose for my blame. I knew that. I'd been in the box toward Chuck for years. My question to Lou was just a way for me to feel justified in my blame. But my need for justification exposed my self-betrayal. Lou had brought me face-to-face with my lie.

Bud spoke up. "I know what you're thinking about, Tom. You've had the misfortune of working with someone who was often in the box. And it was a tough experience. In that kind of situation, it's quite easy to get in the box because the justification is so easy—the other guy's a jerk! But remember, once I get in the box in response, I actually *need* the other guy to keep being a jerk so that I'll remain justified in blaming him for being a jerk. And I don't need to do anything more than get in the box toward him to keep inviting him to be that way. My blame keeps inviting the very thing I'm blaming him for. Because in the box, I need problems.

"Isn't it far better," he went on, "to be able to recognize others' boxes without blaming them for being in the box? After all, I know what it's like to be in the box because I'm there some of the time, too. Out of the box I *understand* what it's like to be in the box. And since, when I'm out of the box, I neither need nor provoke others to be jerks, I can actually ease, rather than exacerbate, tough situations.

"There's another lesson here, of course," he said. "You can see how damaging an in-the-box leader can be. He or she makes it all too easy for others to revert to their boxes as well. The lesson, then, is that you need to be a different kind of leader. That's your obligation as a leader. When you're in the box, people follow you, if at all, only through force or threat of force. But that's not leadership. That's coercion. The leaders that people *choose* to follow are the leaders who are out of the box. Just look back on your life and you'll see that that's so."

Chuck Staehli's face melted from my mind and I saw Amos Page, my first boss at Tetrix. I would have done anything for Amos. He was tough, demanding, and about as out of the box as I could imagine a person being. His enthusiasm for his work and the industry set the course for my whole career. It had been a long time since I'd seen Amos. I made a mental note to look him up and see how he was doing.

"So your success as a leader, Tom, depends on being free of self-betrayal," Bud said. "Only then do you invite others to be free of self-betrayal. Only then are you *creating* leaders yourself—coworkers whom people will respond to, trust, and want to work with. You owe it to your people to be out of the box for them. You owe it to *Zagrum* to be out of the box for them."

Bud stood up. "Let me give you an example of the kind of leader we need you to be," he said, as he began to pace. "My first project as a new attorney was to become an expert in California mobile home law. The results of my research would be crucial to one of the firm's largest clients because that client's expansion plans required the acquisition of large areas of land then occupied by mobile home parks.

"My supervising attorney on the project was a fourth-year attorney named Anita Carlo. As a fourth-year, she was three years away from partnership consideration. First-year attorneys can afford a few mistakes, but fourth-year attorneys don't have that luxury. By then, they're supposed to be seasoned, trustworthy, and competent. Any mistakes at that point in one's law-firm life generally count as heavy negatives when it's time for the partnership vote.

"Well, I threw myself into the project. Over a period of a week or so, I probably became the world's foremost expert on California mobile home law. Yippee, right? I laid everything out in a hefty memo. Anita and the lead partner on the project were happy because the result turned out to be good for our client. Everything was good. I was a hero.

"About two weeks later, Anita and I were working together in her office. Almost in passing she said, 'Oh, by the way, I've been meaning to ask you this: Did you check the pocket parts in all the books you used in your mobile home research?'"

I wasn't familiar with the term Bud had just used. "Pocket parts?" I asked.

"Yeah—have you ever been in a law library?"

"Yes."

"Then you know how thick legal books are," he said.

"Uh-huh."

"Lengthy legal books present a printing challenge that is solved by what are called 'pocket parts.' Let me explain. Legal books are in constant need of revision to reflect the latest developments in the law. In order to avoid frequent reprints of very expensive books, most legal reference books include a pocket in the back where monthly updates are stored."

"So Anita was wondering whether you had checked the most up-to-date versions of the law when you made your analysis," I said.

"Exactly. And when she asked the question, I wanted to run and hide, because in my exuberance I had never thought to check the pockets.

"We ran up to the firm's law library and began pulling all the books I'd used. And guess what? The law had changed. Not just in a marginal way but in a way that changed everything. I had the client running headlong into a public relations and legal nightmare."

"You're kidding," I said.

"Afraid not. Anita and I went back down to her office to give the bad news to Jerry, the lead partner on the project. He was located in a different city, so we had to call him. Now think about it, Tom," he said. "If you were Anita Carlo, under scrutiny for partnership, what would you have told Jerry?"

"Oh, that this first-year guy messed up or something like that," I said. "I would've found *some* way to make sure that he knew it wasn't my fault."

"Me too. But that's not what she did. She said, 'Jerry, you remember that expansion analysis? Well, I made a mistake on it. It turns out that the law has just recently changed, and I missed it. Our expansion strategy is wrong.'

"I was dumfounded listening to her. *I* was the one who'd messed up, not Anita, but she — with much at stake — was taking responsibility for the error. Not even one comment in her conversation pointed to me.

"'What do you mean *you* made a mistake?' I asked her after she hung up. '*I* was the one who didn't check the pocket parts.' This was her response: 'It's true you should've checked them. But I'm your first supervisor, and a number of times during the process I thought that I should remind you to check the pockets, but I never got around to asking until today. If I had asked when I felt I should've, none of this ever would have happened. So you made a mistake, yes. But so did I.'

"Now think about it," Bud continued. "Could Anita have blamed me?"

"Absolutely."

"And she would've been justified in blaming me, wouldn't she?" Bud asked. "Because, after all, I really *did* make a mistake. I *was* blameworthy."

"Yeah, I guess that's right," I said.

"But notice," Bud said with feeling, "she didn't *need* to blame me — even though I made a mistake — because she herself wasn't in the box. Out of the box she had no need for justification."

Bud paused for a moment and sat back down. "And here's the interesting thing: Do you suppose that by claiming responsibility for her mistake, Anita made me feel less or more responsible for my own?"

"Oh, more," I said.

"That's right," Bud agreed. "A hundred times more. By refusing to look for justification for her relatively little mistake, she invited me to take responsibility for my own major one. From that moment on, I would've gone through a brick wall for Anita Carlo.

"But think how different it would've been," he said, "if she *had* blamed me. How do you suppose I would've reacted had Anita blamed me when she talked to Jerry?"

"Well, I don't know what you might've done *exactly*, but you probably would've started to find some weaknesses in her that made her hard to work for, for one thing."

"Exactly. And both Anita and I would've then been focused on ourselves instead of what we needed to focus on at that point more than ever—the result for the client."

"And that," Lou said, joining back in, "is exactly what I realized my problem was as I sat in Arizona learning this material. I had failed, in all kinds of ways, to do my best to help Zagrum and its employees to achieve results. In other words," he said, pointing to the board, "I'd betrayed my sense of what I needed to do for others in the venture. And in doing that, I buried myself in the box. I wasn't focused on results at all; I was just focused on myself. And as a result of that self-betrayal, I blamed others for everything. That picture there," he said, pointing again at the diagram, "that was me. I saw everyone in the company as problems and saw myself as the victim of their incompetence.

"But in that moment of realization—a moment that one would expect would be dark and depressing—in that moment I felt the first happiness and hope about my company that I'd had in months. Still very unsure of where this would end up, I had an overwhelming feeling of something—a first thing— that I needed to do. Something that I had to do if I was to move forward out of the box.

"I had to go see Kate."

23 Birth of a Leader

"Carol and I left Arizona the following night on the red-eye," Lou said. "We'd planned to spend a few days of R&R in San Diego before going home, but our plans had all changed. I'd heard that Kate would be starting her new job in the Bay Area in just a few days. I desperately hoped that I could catch her before she left. I needed to deliver something to her," he said, looking past me out the window again. "I needed to take her a ladder."

"A ladder?" I asked.

"Yes, a ladder. One of the last things I did to Kate before she left," he recalled, "was demand that a ladder be removed from her sales area. Her department had decided to use the ladder as a visual aid in promoting some sales goals. I thought it was a stupid idea and told her so when she asked me about it. But they went ahead and did it anyway. Later that night, I told the custodial staff to remove the ladder from the premises. Three days later, she and the other four members of the March Meltdown group gave me their two-months' notice. I had them removed by our security staff within an hour— didn't even allow them to go back into their offices alone. *Anyone who turned on me like that can't be trusted*, I told myself. That was the last time I had seen or spoken with Kate.

"I can't explain it, but I just knew that I needed to take her a ladder. It was a symbol of so much. And so I did.

"Carol and I arrived back at JFK at about 6:00 AM on Sunday. I had the limo driver drop Carol off at home and then take me by the office, where I rummaged through a half-dozen or so supply closets before I found a ladder. We tied it to the top of the car and headed up to Kate's place in Litchfield. It was about 9:30 or so when I rang her doorbell, the ladder laid across my back.

"The door opened and I saw Kate, her eyes in wide surprise at the sight of me. 'Now before you say anything, Kate,' I said, 'I have something I've got to say, even though I don't know how I can ever begin to say it. First of all, I'm sorry for just barging in on you on a Sunday morning, but it couldn't wait. I . . . umm, I . . . '

"All of a sudden, Kate just busted up laughing. 'Sorry, Lou,' she said, doubled over against the doorjamb. 'I know you must have something serious to say or you wouldn't be here, but the sight of you hunched over with that ladder is just too much to take. Here, let me help you put it down.'

"'Yeah, about the ladder,' I said, 'that's as good a place to start as any. I never should've done what I did. I don't know why I did it, to be honest. I shouldn't have even cared.'

"Kate had stopped laughing by then and was listening intently. 'Look, Kate,' I said, 'I've been a real jackass. You know that. Everyone knows it. But I didn't know it until two days ago. Or I couldn't see it, anyway. But I can sure see it now. And the sight of what I've done to the people I care about most in my life terrifies me—and that includes you.'

"She just stood there, listening. I couldn't tell what she was thinking.

"'I know that you've got something really good lined up,' I continued. 'And I'd never expect you to come back to Zagrum—not after the way I've been. But I'm here to plead with you. There's something I've got to talk to you about, and then, if you tell me to, I'll leave and never bother you again. But I see what I've done to mess this all up for everybody, and

I think I have an idea of how to put it back together. I've got to talk to you.'

"She stepped back from the door. 'Okay,' she said. 'I'll listen.'

"Over the next three hours I tried my best to share with her what I'd learned about the box and everything else over the prior couple of days. I think I botched it pretty badly," Lou said, looking at me with a smile. "But it wasn't so important what I said. She could tell, whatever it was I was talking about, that I meant it.

"Finally she said, 'Okay, Lou. But I have a question: If I were to come back, how would I know that this isn't just some temporary change? Why should I take the chance?'

"I think my shoulders hunched a bit. I didn't know what to say. 'That's a good question,' I said finally. 'I wish I could tell you not to worry. But I know myself better than that. And so do you. That's one of the things that I want to talk to you about. I need your help.'

"I explained to her a rudimentary plan. 'Two things need to happen,' I told her. 'First, we need to institute a process in our company where we help people to see how they're in the box and are therefore not focusing on results. Second—and this is key, especially for me personally—we need to institute a system of focusing on results that keeps us *out of* the box much more than we have been: a way of thinking, a way of measuring, a way of reporting, a way of working. For once we're out of the box,' I told her, 'there are a lot of things we can do to help keep us out while going forward. We need to institute such a system at Zagrum.'

" 'Do you have some ideas about that?' she asked.

" 'Yes, a few. But I need your help, Kate,' I said. 'Together we could figure out the best way to do it. No one I know would be able to do it as well as you could.'

"She sat there in thought. 'I'm not sure,' she said slowly. 'I'm going to have to think about it. Can I call you?'

" 'Absolutely. I'll be waiting by the phone.' "

"As you can gather," Lou said, "she called. I was given a second chance. And the Zagrum you've been admiring over these many years has been the result of that second chance.

"We made a lot of mistakes as we got restarted together. The only thing we did really well at the outset was to cover with our people the ideas you've learned over these last two days. We didn't necessarily know all the implications in the workplace, so at first we stayed at the level of the general ideas. And you know something? It made a big difference. Just what Bud's done for you these two days—that alone, when learned by people in a common enterprise, has a powerful, lasting effect. We know because we've measured the results over time.

"But over the last 20 or so years, we've become much more sophisticated in the specific application of the material to business. As we became more out of the box as a company, we were able to identify and develop a specific plan of action that minimizes the basic workplace self-betrayal that we've been talking about. Right out of the chute, when people generally are still out of the box toward their coworkers and the company, we introduce our people to this way of working together."

Lou paused, and Bud jumped in. "Our effort now is in three phases," he said. "Yesterday and today, you've begun what we call our Phase 1 curriculum. It's all we had in the beginning, and it alone has tremendous impact. It's the foundation for everything that comes later. It's what makes our results here possible. Our work in Phases 2 and 3 will build on what we've covered by plugging you into a concrete and systematic way of focusing on and accomplishing results—an 'accountability transformation system' that minimizes self-betrayal at work and maximizes the company's bottom line. And it does this in a way that greatly reduces common organizational people problems."

"Accountability transformation system?" I asked.

Bud nodded. "Who are you focused on when you're in the box?"

"Myself mostly."

"And *what* are you focused on when you're in the box?"

I thought about it for a moment, and then said, "On being justified."

"What if all the workers in an organization held themselves accountable for achieving a particular, concrete result? If they were truly accountable for this, would they be justified if they failed to accomplish that result?"

I shook my head. "Probably not."

"So they would therefore be focused on achieving a result rather than on being justified. Right?"

"I suppose so," I said, wondering where Bud was going with this.

"And what if this result, by its very nature, required the workers to be thinking of others?"

I didn't answer immediately.

"Think about it," he continued. "If everyone was focused on *others*, who would they *not* be focused on?"

"Themselves?" I ventured.

"Exactly. An in-the-box organization is filled with people who are focused on themselves and on being justified. Imagine, in contrast, an organization where everyone is focused on others and on achieving results."

"It would be an out-of-the-box organization," I said.

"Exactly. And that is what our accountability transformation system is designed to create. In a disciplined, sustained
fashion, we keep people focused on results and on others.
The culture of blame that is so prevalent in organizations
is replaced with a culture of deep responsibility-taking and
accountability. People who focus on themselves and on being
justified don't make it here."

"What about seeing those underachievers as people?" I
quipped, before I could stop myself.

"Letting people go is a behavior," Bud responded. "There
are two ways to do it."

"I know, I know," I said, attempting to cover myself.

"And in the unfortunate case where we have to let someone go," he continued without pause, "we aim to let a *person*
go, not an object. It's an entirely different thing."

I nodded, now clearly realizing that my future at Zagrum
depended on getting this right. "So what do I need to do to
begin applying this accountability system?" I asked. "I'm
ready to move on to Phase 2."

"No you're not," Bud said, smiling. "Not quite."

"I'm not?"

"No. Because although you now understand what the
foundational self-betrayal at work is, you don't yet understand
the extent to which you are in it. You don't yet understand the
extent to which you've been failing to focus on results."

I felt my face begin to slacken again, and I realized in that
moment that I hadn't felt that defensive sensation since the
previous morning. The thought seemed to rescue me, and I
returned again to openness.

"But you're no different from anyone else on that score," Bud said, with a warm smile. "You'll see it soon enough. In fact, I have some material for you to read, and then I'd like to meet with you again in a week. We'll need about an hour."

"Okay. I'll look forward to it," I said.

"And then the labor will begin," Bud added. "You'll need to rethink your work, learn to measure things you never knew needed measuring, and help and report to people in ways you've never thought of. You will learn to hold yourself accountable in deep and disciplined ways. As your manager, I will help you do all this. And you, as a manager, will learn how to help your people do the same. You will discover, through it all, that there is no better way to work, or to live."

Bud stood up. "All of this together makes Zagrum what it is, Tom. We're glad you're a part of it. By the way, in addition to your reading, I have some homework for you."

"Okay," I said, wondering what it might be.

"I want you to think of your time working with Chuck Staehli."

"Staehli?" I asked, surprised.

"Yes. I want you to think about how and whether you really focused on results during the time you worked with him. I want you to consider whether you were open or closed to correction, whether you actively sought to learn and enthusiastically taught when you could have. Whether you held yourself fully accountable in your work, whether you took or shifted responsibility when things went wrong. Whether you moved quickly to solutions or instead found perverse value in problems. Whether you earned in those around you—including Chuck Staehli—their trust.

"And as you think about that, I want you to keep continually in your mind the ideas we've covered. But I want you to do it in a particular kind of way." Bud pulled something from his briefcase. "A little knowledge can be a dangerous thing, Tom. You can use this material to blame just as well as you can use anything else. Merely *knowing* the material doesn't get you out of the box. *Living* it does. And we're not living it if we're using it to diagnose others. Rather, we're living it when we're using it to learn how we can be more helpful to others — even to others like Chuck Staehli.

"Here are some things to keep in mind while you're trying to do just that," he said, handing me a card.

This is what it said:

KNOWING THE MATERIAL

- Self-betrayal leads to self-deception and "the box."

- When you're in the box, you can't focus on results.

- Your influence and success will depend on being out of the box.

- You get out of the box as you cease resisting other people.

LIVING THE MATERIAL

- Don't try to be perfect. Do try to be better.

- Don't use the vocabulary—"the box," and so on—with people who don't already know it. Do use the principles in your own life.

- Don't look for others' boxes. Do look for your own.

- Don't accuse others of being in the box. Do try to stay out of the box yourself.

- Don't give up on yourself when you discover you've been in the box. Do keep trying.

- Don't deny that you've been in the box when you have been. Do apologize; then just keep marching forward, trying to be more helpful to others in the future.

- Don't focus on what others are doing wrong. Do focus on what you can do right to help.

- Don't worry whether others are helping you. Do worry whether you are helping others.

"Okay, Bud. This will be helpful. Thanks," I said, slipping the card into my briefcase.

"Sure," Bud said. "And I look forward to seeing you again next week."

I nodded, then stood up and turned to thank Lou.

"Before you go, Tom," said Lou, "I'd like to share one last thing with you."

"Please," I said.

"My boy—Cory—do you remember him?"

"Yeah."

"Well, two months after Carol and I watched him drive away, we rode in that same van to the remote wilderness that had been Cory's home for those nine or so weeks. We were going out to meet him, to live with him for a few days, and then to bring him home. I don't think I've ever been so nervous.

"I had written him frequently in the weeks he was gone. The program leaders delivered letters to the kids every Tuesday. I had poured out my soul to him in those letters, and slowly, like a young foal taking his first uncertain steps into a stream, he began to open himself to me.

"I had discovered through those letters a boy I never knew I had. He was full of questions and insights. I marveled at the depth and feeling within his heart. But most especially, there was a peace singing through his prose that had the effect of calming the heart of a father who feared that he'd driven away a son. Every letter sent, and every letter received, was a source of healing.

"As we covered the last few miles to the rendezvous point, I was overcome with the thought of what almost was—a bitterly divided father and son who had risked never knowing each other. At the brink of war—a war whose effects might have been felt for generations—we were saved by a miracle.

"Driving around the last dusty hill, I saw about a quarter of a mile away the dirtiest, scraggliest-looking group of kids that I'd ever seen—clothes worn and torn, stringy beards, hair two months' past due for clippers. But as we neared them, out of that pack flew a lone boy, a boy whose now-lean figure I yet recognized through the dirt and grime. 'Stop the car. Stop the car!' I yelled at the driver. And out I darted to meet my son.

"He reached me in an instant and leaped into my arms, tears streaming down his dusty face. Through the sobs I heard, 'I'll never let you down again, Dad. I'll never let you down again.'"

Lou stopped, choking back the memory of the moment.

"That he should feel that for me," he continued, more slowly, "the one who had let *him* down, melted my heart.

"'And I won't let you down again, either, Son,' I said."

Lou paused, separating himself from his memory. Then he rose from his chair and looked at me with his kindly eyes.

"Tom," he said, putting his hands on my shoulders, "the thing that divides fathers from sons, husbands from wives, neighbors from neighbors—the same thing divides coworkers from coworkers as well. Companies fail for the same reason families do. And why should we be surprised to discover that it's so? For those coworkers I'm resisting are themselves fathers, mothers, sons, daughters, brothers, sisters.

"A family, a company—both are organizations of *people*. That's what we know and live by at Zagrum.

"Just remember," he added, "we won't know who we work and live with—whether it be Bud, Kate, your wife, your son, even someone like Chuck Staehli—until we leave the box and join them."

Resources for Readers

Research about Self-Deception in Organizations

As we discuss in *Leadership and Self-Deception*, self-deception is the most debilitating of organizational issues. This is so because problems can't be solved if those responsible for the problems remain resistant to the possibility that they may be at fault. We share a somewhat humorous yet troubling example of this issue in our book *The Outward Mindset*. The story seems particularly relevant here, as it is about the man who was the inspiration for the Lou character in *Leadership and Self-Deception*. His name was Jack Hauck.

Jack Hauck was the founder and longtime CEO of a company called Tubular Steel, a St. Louis–based national distributor of steel and carbon products. Years ago, Tubular had engaged one of the world's best-known consultants to help it overcome the toxic infighting that plagued the senior management team and stymied the growth of the entire company. After months of trying one approach after another without success, Jack asked this consultant if he knew of any other approach the company could try. The consultant was acquainted with Arbinger's work and recommended that Jack explore our ideas.

During our first meeting with Jack and his team, we focused on helping each executive team member reassess his or her contribution to the challenges the company faced by carefully considering the following statement: *As far as I am concerned, the problem is me.*

Jack was eager to solve his company's problems, and he saw real promise in this approach. However, he remained blind to how he was failing to apply our work to himself. At the end of the first day with his team, feeling energized by the headway he thought they were making, he stood up to reaffirm his commitment to the effort. "I want you all to get the message," he said. "I'm going to have posters made and put up all over the building." Then, pointing his finger at the assembled executives and officers, he said, "Don't forget: As far as you are concerned, the problem is you!"

You can imagine the reaction of his team members. In the very moment Jack thought he had gotten the point he had completely missed it. This blindness to personal responsibility is the problem of self-deception. Jack gradually was able to overcome this blindness and begin to see more straightforwardly and clearly. As a result, his company completely turned around, even in the face of a difficult economy in which the market for its products was collapsing. Over a three-year period, the market size for Tubular Steel's products had shrunk from 10 million tons to 6 million tons, but the company grew its revenue over that same period from $30 million to $100 million. Tubular Steel was able to achieve this growth only because the team members were able to evaluate, quantify, and address the problem of self-deception that had been holding them back.

Our research has revealed an interesting way to assess the level of self-deception in an organization. For years we have had participants in our workshops anonymously rate their own and their organizations' mindsets on a continuum from 1 to 10—from what we call "entirely inward" to "entirely outward." (An inward mindset equates to being "in the box" and an outward mindset to being "out of the box.") Interestingly, people rate themselves much higher on this continuum—that is, as much more *outward*—than they rate their organizations. We find it interesting, as well, that this result surprises almost nobody! People nearly universally expect that they and others will rate themselves more highly than they will rate their employer organizations. Why is this? Why do people think more highly of themselves than they do their organizations, and why does everybody know that this is how everybody thinks?

The math, of course, doesn't work. A company that truly deserves a rating of 4 out of 10 on the mindset continuum, for example, can't be populated by people who, on average, have a rating of 8. When we point this out, people tend to laugh nervously (again, almost universally). The difference between how we rate ourselves and how we rate others is what we call the "self-deception gap." Self-deception is what explains this inflated view of ourselves relative to others.

Our research shows that people intuitively know of the problem of self-deception. They know of it not primarily because they recognize it in themselves but because they observe in others the tendency to overinflate performance relative to results, and they observe how people explain this difference by blaming others for problems rather than taking responsibility themselves. An interesting aspect of self-deception is that people who observe and recognize these behaviors in others are no less likely than others to do the same things themselves. However, they believe their own self-assessments are more accurate than the overinflated self-assessments of their colleagues! Like Jack Hauck early on at Tubular Steel (or Lou Herbert), they see the problem; they just don't see it in themselves.

This nearly universal self-deception gap is reaffirmed in formal assessments we administer with our client organizations. A twenty-question survey instrument called the Arbinger Mindset Assessment measures in a more detailed way where respondents rate their organizations' mindset and where they rate their own.

The mindset assessment asks questions that measure characteristics such as awareness, helpfulness, accountability, alignment, collaboration, self-correction, coordination, inclusivity, generosity, transparency, results focus, openness, appreciation, recognition, empowerment, initiative, engagement, and safety. Looking at these various elements and averaging results across industries, we have found that people rate their colleagues in their organizations at an average of 4.8 on the continuum and themselves at 6.8, which is to say that individuals rate themselves as 40 percent better than the rest of the people in their organizations across these characteristics.

The self-deception gap between respondents' self-views as compared to their views of others narrows with respect to one of the characteristics in the mindset assessment. In our experience, this characteristic is the single biggest indicator of mindset in an organization. We call this characteristic "horizontal alignment." It is a measure of the extent of understanding people have about the objectives, needs, and challenges of those lateral to them in their organizations.

The reason why horizontal alignment is such a helpful indicator of mindset is that a hyperactive self-interest, which is what drives someone who is in the box (or who has an inward mindset), doesn't incentivize a person to build awareness about the objectives, needs, and challenges of his or her lateral coworkers. Self-interest may well drive someone to learn about the objectives, needs, and challenges of his or her boss, but an inward-mindset orientation won't invite the same effort toward people situated horizontally from oneself in an organization. From the perspective of an inward mindset, that kind of effort doesn't seem to be relevant and seems unlikely to make much of a personal difference. The inward-mindset perspective is wrong on both counts, but the blindness perpetuated by that mindset obscures reality.

Interestingly, people score their own and their organizations' horizontal alignment lower than any other characteristic in the assessment. The self-deception gap still exists for this element, but that gap is 50 percent smaller than for the other elements. This result indicates something quite important: Horizontal alignment is so poor in most organizations that, even when suffering from self-deception, people find it hard to obscure the fact that they themselves aren't very good at it. Accordingly, efforts to increase horizontal awareness within and across teams is a key strategy both for helping people become aware of the inwardness that has characterized an organization and for helping individuals, teams, and entire organizations break free from the box. This is such an important strategy that Arbinger equips clients with a number of tools to help them increase horizontal awareness and alignment in their organizations and reduce the competing objectives and silos that are characteristic of organizations with poor horizontal awareness.

How to Measure the Self-Deception Gap with the Arbinger Mindset Assessment

The Arbinger Mindset Assessment described above is available for your use. You may take the assessment free of charge at www.arbinger.com. It is a 20-question instrument that should take you less than five minutes to complete. You will receive an automated analysis of your and your organization's mindsets based on your answers.

If you wish to get data on a team, department, or entire organization, Arbinger can grant you access to the group-level instrument, which will yield a group-level assessment that will include, among other data points, a measure of the self-deception gap in the organization. Contact Arbinger to set up a group-level assessment.

From Way-of-Being Change to Mindset Change

In *Leadership and Self-Deception,* we describe two completely different life experiences—a self-deceived, *in-the-box* experience and an un-self-deceived, *out-of-the-box* experience. From reading the book, you know that one of the key differences between these two experiences of life is the way we see and experience other people: When we are in the box, we experience others not as people with their own lives but as objects within *our* lives. When we experience others in these two ways, we experience *ourselves* differently as well. The choice to see another as either a person or an object is a choice between whether we will see and experience ourselves and others truthfully or erroneously.

One's experiences of oneself and others are so radically different between these two ways that philosophers call them different "ways of being." The choice to move from living in the box to living out of the box (or vice versa) amounts to a radical shift in one's way of being in the world, which is to say that it changes not only one's behavior but also one's thoughts, emotions, interpretations of events, and views of the past, present, and future.

In the years since *Leadership and Self-Deception* was first published, our work with clients has caused us to continue to refine the terms we use to make a rigorously logical philosophical work an equally powerful practical one. We have discovered that clients are able to understand and apply the concepts we teach more easily if we characterize our work in terms of "mindset change" rather than "way-of-being change." Perhaps this is because the term "way of being," while accurately communicating the foundational depth of the issue we are taking on, also communicates a kind of gravity that seems difficult to change. The term "mindset," while also carrying the idea of foundational change, sounds and feels inherently changeable, which it is.

As part of this developmental process, a number of years ago we began talking in terms of "changing mindset" rather than "changing way of being." Specifically, we began talking about helping individuals, teams, and organizations shift from inward-mindset (in-the-box) orientations to outward-mindset (out-of-the-box) orientations. We soon learned how helpful it was to our clients to characterize the change we are seeking in this way.

The ideas we share in this book still hold true nearly 20 years later. Terms like "in the box" and "out of the box" have entered the public lexicon and helped hundreds of thousands—even millions—of people. The book's continued and increasing popularity—early on as a word-of-mouth phenomenon and now as one of the bestselling leadership books of all time—proves the timeless power of the ideas. As you encounter Arbinger's work in its most recent book, *The Outward Mindset*, the connections between the books will remain clear when you remember that the in-the-box way of being is what we now often call an "inward mindset," and the out-of-the-box way of being is what we call an "outward mindset."

Our *mission* is to turn the world outward—one person, team, and organization at a time.

How to Use Leadership and Self-Deception

We have been gratified and amazed at the range of uses that people have made of *Leadership and Self-Deception*. Although it is styled as a book about business, readers have recognized that its foundational ideas apply to every aspect of life—from building a lasting marriage, for example, to raising children, and from driving organizational success to achieving personal fulfillment and happiness. Whether at work or at home, the applications are wide and various.

It has been interesting to hear from readers about ways they are using the book. We have found that its many uses fall within five broad categories of human and organizational experience. The first of these areas of application is in hiring. Many organizations use the book as a vital part of their applicant screening and hiring process. They require potential hires to read the book, and then they use post-reading discussions with these applicants to evaluate key characteristics of success that are difficult to assess using normal hiring processes.

A second broad area of application is what you might think of as leadership and team building. This application is pretty clear from the book itself, as the degree to which one is in the box toward others has huge implications about that person's ability to cooperate with and lead others. This is as true at home as it is at work.

A third area of application is conflict resolution. If you think about it, the one thing every party in a conflict is sure of is that the conflict is someone else's fault. This means that there can be no lasting solution to a given conflict unless those who are responsible break through the blindness of self-deception and begin to consider their own culpability. This, too, is as true at home as it is at work.

A fourth area of application is presented near the end of the book. The self-deception solution forms a foundation upon which organizations of all types can build robust systems of accountability and responsibility-taking. The reason for this is that, once out of the box, people have no need to blame or to shirk responsibility. Getting out of the box therefore opens organizations to a level of disciplined initiative-taking that box-laden organizations can't achieve.

A final area of application might broadly be called "personal growth and development." Getting out of the box improves everything in life — for example, thoughts about others, feelings about oneself, hopes for the future, and the ability to make changes in the present. For these reasons, the book has become very popular among personal coaches, counselors, and therapists.

In summary, then, the myriad ways in which people have used this book and its ideas fall within five broad areas of application: (1) applicant screening and hiring, (2) leadership and team building, (3) conflict resolution, (4) accountability transformation, and (5) personal growth and development. We discuss in more detail below some specific uses people have been making of this book in each of these areas.

Applicant Screening and Hiring

Many organizations utilize the book in their hiring practices. Prospective employees are required to read the book as part of the application process. Interviewers then emphasize the importance of the book's companion ideas of seeing others as people and focusing on results. They stress that making things more difficult for others and treating others as objects is not tolerated and will be grounds for termination. This establishes clear expectations even before a person is hired and helps to filter out individuals who are unwilling to commit to the out-of-the-box way of working.

Here is what one of our client organizations wrote about this use of the book:

> We require all applicants to read and come prepared to discuss *Leadership and Self-Deception* at the second interview. Specifically, we ask them to share what discoveries they made while reading the book. It helps us to more quickly assess the degree to which someone is willing to consider their contribution to problems they encounter in their work or with others—a key predictor of those who succeed in our company. Screening in this way has helped us achieve industry-leading low turnover among business unit leaders that has become one of our trademark competitive advantages. A careful reading of the book also helps us to better train leaders to recognize the signs and symptoms of resistant tendencies of potential new hires, which helps us to avoid costly new hires: defensiveness, inflated view of their own contribution to their success, blame, indulgence, etc. We

take this so seriously that we provide what we consider ongoing 'graduate level' training on applied *Leadership and Self-Deception* principles in hiring to ensure that our business unit leaders develop this crucial leadership competency.

Leadership and Team Building

We have heard from companies too numerous to count how simply sharing *Leadership and Self-Deception* with their workers has dramatically improved cooperation and teamwork across their organizations. Some of these organizations mandate or encourage all their people to read the book, while others concentrate on managers of a certain rank. Some organizations follow up with formal and informal discussion groups where colleagues help each other to apply the ideas to their work situations. Many of these organizations also engage Arbinger's help, and we support their efforts with training and consultation around the leadership and team building applications of our work.

The results are dramatic. From line leaders to global CEOs, we frequently hear how the book has totally changed the way these leaders see themselves and interact with their teams. We have heard from many people, for example, about how their company CEO or immediate supervisor has improved as dramatically as Lou improved in the book. One leader wrote, "We are not going into the box as often, and when we do get in the box, we come out much more quickly because we recognize the red flags and feelings that coincide with the box. Our meetings are less contentious and people are more patient with each other. It's as if a kind of oil, of sorts, has flowed over all of us and lubricated the company, enabling us to be more honest about ourselves and more respectful of others."

One company wrote to tell us that when they hire new business unit leaders, they engage them in a condensed version of Bud's encounters with Tom in the book. They, like the characters in *Leadership and Self-Deception*, affectionately call these "Bud Meetings." In these meetings, they teach their people, among other things, about the problem of self-deception and its impact on one's work, stress the need to be able to focus fully on results rather than on oneself and justification, and orient their people to the way they will be required to focus on results that is based on the teachings in the book.

Uses of the book for team building and leadership purposes have not stopped at company doors, however. People who read the book for work typically bring it home and pass it around in their families as well. Couples and families often read the book together and apply their learning to their family situations. We often hear from people who say that their home lives have been greatly enriched by the book. At the risk of sounding overly dramatic, one executive reported that the book saved his son's life. Another who suffered from depression confided that it very likely saved his own.

One executive shared the following after reading the book:

> I am afraid that my words won't convey the impact three hours of reading has just had on my life, my leadership, and my future. I have to tell you that there haven't been too many life-changing moments while I have been reading, but today I had one. This book is so compelling that I handed it to my wife when I came home and feel like I need to share it with my entire team. I'm going to have a book

reading with my team and then get into a discussion about it. I'll probably need to read it a couple more times myself, though, as I'm sure I don't get it yet . . . just like Tom.

We could go on, as the uses people have made of the book to build relationships and increase cooperation are nearly endless. When using the book in this way, however, we have learned an important tip: The book's title can seem accusing. For this reason, it is often helpful when giving the book to another to say something like, "Here is a book that will help you to see how to deal with me when I'm really being a jerk." There's nothing accusing in that invitation. People will read it and learn whatever it is they are prepared to learn.

Conflict Resolution

The police department in one of the major cities in the United States has used the ideas in *Leadership and Self-Deception* and its companion book, *The Anatomy of Peace*, to completely change the way they interact with the public in highly volatile situations. For example, when making a drug bust, their understanding of the importance of their way of being and seeing others as people has given them a means of quickly de-escalating tensions and restoring calm and order, minimizing trauma to innocent parties while quickly securing the cooperation of their targets.

This approach combines the ideas regarding being out of the box from *Leadership and Self-Deception* with the Influence Pyramid from *The Anatomy of Peace*. Once a door is broken in, for example, and the suspects are apprehended, the police officers immediately begin to attend to the needs of the suspects and others who might be on the scene. Do they need some water, for example, or do they need to use the rest-room? Are they comfortable? Is there anything else the officers can do for them? And so on. They report that since they have begun focusing on seeing all the people they encounter—even suspects—as people, community complaints about police behavior have dropped essentially to zero. Although this approach may make for less dramatic TV than the public is accustomed to seeing, it has proved to make for far more effective law enforcement.

Many judges in mediation situations are requiring the parties to read *Leadership and Self-Deception* or *The Anatomy of Peace* before proceeding with their mediations. We have heard many stories of parties who settled their differences on their own after reading one or both of these books. Even where this doesn't happen, the concepts in the books provide a common language and understanding that enables the mediation to proceed effectively. In addition, judges and mediators say that the books equip them to remain out of the box—and therefore be more effective—even when the parties are tearing into each other and things are most difficult. These professionals have discovered that being out of the box is the quality that determines the helpfulness of every mediation skill they have ever learned.

The book is used not only in mediations, but also more broadly within the legal justice system. One practitioner wrote, "Imagine using these concepts to help a client see that a problem previously viewed as insurmountable is actually amenable to a solution short of litigation. Or imagine using the ideas to help a client understand why a negotiation tanked, and to suggest a party-to-party approach that could get it back on track." As an example of this kind of application, after reading *Leadership and Self-Deception*, a company CEO called his counterpart at a supplier that his company was suing. He suggested that they meet to see if they could resolve their differences. Not only did they resolve their differences without going to court, but they agreed to keep doing business together!

The book's utility in conflict situations is not limited to the legal justice system, of course. We frequently hear from people who say that their marriage was saved by their reading the book, for example, or that the book enabled them to resolve differences with a boss or colleague. A group of teachers at a school reported that their conflict-laden work environment was transformed into a culture of cooperation merely by having everyone read the book and then meet over a number of sessions to talk about what they had learned. Similarly, the leaders of a major US corporation were able to resolve a costly labor/management dispute after they and their counterparts at the union read the book.

The reason *Leadership and Self-Deception* and *The Anatomy of Peace* have been so instrumental in helping people to resolve conflict is that they open readers to how they have helped to create the very problems they have attributed to others. This is the essence of the self-deception solution— discovering how each of us has the problem of not knowing we have a problem. This is the realization that makes conflict resolution possible.

Accountability Transformation

Managers often use the book to help rehabilitate employees who will lose their jobs unless some serious changes are made. In many cases, the book has helped these employees to see problems they had never been able to see and to take the corrective steps necessary to save their careers.

For example, a gentleman in his 50s had worked in the same company for nearly three decades. Although he was talented, interpersonal problems kept him from moving up in the company. As he was passed over for promotions year after year, he grew angry. Finally, a young man a full generation younger was promoted to be his boss, and the man's anger turned to rage. His former boss gave him a copy of *Leadership and Self-Deception* in the hopes that the man would see himself clearly for perhaps the very first time.

The man read the book twice. The first time through, he thought it naïvely ignored what to him was the dominant issue in most companies—politics. On the second reading, however, he started to open up to the possibility that he was at least partially responsible for his fate. He began asking some of his longtime colleagues for feedback about how he affected those around him. Unlike in years past, he just listened without trying to defend himself. He was humbled by what he heard and began to hold himself accountable for issues he had always blamed on others.

A position as a temporary supervisor of a historically low-performing team opened up. He asked for the opportunity to lead that group. His first day on the job, he told his team: "I can promise one thing to you. Every day, I will try my hardest to see and treat you as people. You can count on that. If I don't, you come and let me know so I can change." The team broke production records the first month. The next month they were the only team in the company to exceed their goals. They continued improving every month thereafter, and the man's peer supervisors wondered how it had all happened.

What happened, of course, was that the man began holding himself accountable rather than waiting around for others to hold him accountable. And that single change changed everything. It is the transformation that *Leadership and Self-Deception* invites.

In this spirit, one CEO, after reading *Leadership and Self-Deception*, fired himself and hired a more able person to take his place. Another, instead of writing a blistering memo that would have made a whole division of his company into scapegoats, wrote an apology to his company for mistakes he himself had made that had set them up to fail. The company rallied behind him with new commitment and vigor.

The book led another CEO to institute a new way of tackling problems in the company. Whereas before, he would go to the person he thought was causing the problem and demand that that person fix it, the CEO began to consider how he himself might have contributed to the problem. He then convened a meeting including each person in the chain of command down to the level where the problem was manifest. He began the meeting by identifying the problem. He laid out all the ways he thought he had negatively contributed to the culture that had produced the problem and proposed a plan to rectify his contributions to the problem. He invited the person directly below him to do the same thing. And so on down the line. By the time it got to the person most immediately responsible for the problem, that person publicly took responsibility for his contributions to the problem and then proposed a plan for what he would do about it. In this way, a problem that had gone on literally for years was solved nearly overnight when the leaders stopped simply assigning responsibility and began holding themselves strictly accountable. This is now the model in that company for solving every problem encountered.

This level of personal accountability in an organization should be every leader's dream. What our experience tells us, and what we try to communicate in this book, is that in order to move from merely dreaming about a culture of responsibility-taking and accountability to actually experiencing it, the accountability has to start with the leader—whether that leader is the CEO, a division VP, a line manager, or a parent. The most effective leaders lead in this single way: by holding themselves more accountable than all.

Personal Growth and Development

Leadership and Self-Deception was discovered early on by prominent members of the personal and executive coaching professions. It is now a staple book for many coaching programs, as coaches find it to be a highly valuable tool in helping their clients with personal growth issues. The book is also widely used by therapists and counselors, as mental health practitioners find that the model connects with people in ways that significantly improve the effectiveness of their services.

The book is used as a foundational text in many university and business school courses as well. Professors find that the ideas in the book provide an important foundation for many areas of study—from ethics to business management to organizational behavior to psychology.

A prominent pharmacy school in the United States has all of its first-year students read the book for orientation. Faculty members then meet in two-hour sessions with the students to discuss the concepts and their relevance to the profession.

Another university offers *Leadership and Self-Deception* and *The Anatomy of Peace*, along with a supporting course, to all of its students as part of an effort to build community across cultures. A prominent law school utilizes Arbinger's books as the curriculum for a semester-long course on law and leadership.

Many treatment programs supply copies of the books to the family members of their clients in order to help those key caregivers to reengage with their sons and daughters and other loved ones in more healthy and loving ways.

We hear frequently from readers who engage with others around these materials. These engagements take many forms. In Japan, for example, "out of the box" clubs in cities around the country provide a space where readers can help each other around these concepts. In the United States, initiatives on college campuses give students ways to gather and discuss these ideas. Arbinger offers a global community on the web as well, through its portal at arbinger.com, where readers and Arbinger practitioners from around the world can explore the theoretical and practical implications of the work.

Those who want to take the next step can engage an Arbinger coach for personal help in applying *Leadership and Self-Deception* in their daily and professional lives or can engage Arbinger for team- or organization-level change efforts. Services can be arranged through Arbinger's website or by calling Arbinger directly at 801-447-9244. In addition, public workshops are available in cities around the world. Longer advanced training also is available. Training options are detailed on Arbinger's website at www.arbinger.com.

Introducing The Anatomy of Peace—World #1 Bestseller in the Categories of War and Peace and Conflict Resolution

Leadership and Self-Deception is one of the top 50 bestselling leadership books of all time. Its prequel, *The Anatomy of Peace*, has been number one or two on the Amazon bestseller list in the War and Peace and Conflict Resolution categories for more than a decade. That means that every hour of every day for over 10 years, *The Anatomy of Peace* has been the best-selling book in its category. Few books in history can make that claim.

The Anatomy of Peace is the story of how Lou Herbert learned the ideas that ended up transforming his company by the time we encounter that company in *Leadership and Self-Deception*. Before his company transformed, Lou transformed, as did his family relationships—both with his wife, Carol, and with their son, Cory. *The Anatomy of Peace* tells the story of how those transformations happened.

The events in *The Anatomy of Peace* take place some 20 years prior to the events in *Leadership and Self-Deception*, just two weeks after five of Zagrum Company's executives, including Kate Stenarude, had quit. At that time of professional duress, Lou and Carol flew to Arizona to put Cory into a court-ordered treatment program. In their minds, it was a last-ditch effort to fix him. The treatment program was headed by a Palestinian and an Israeli in a business partnership. They were once bitter enemies, the historical divide between their peoples running down the center of their respective hearts. But they had overcome their histories and figured out how to help others overcome their divisions as well.

As Lou and Carol came under the tutelage of these two men, they learned that Cory wasn't the only person who needed to make changes. Their marriage, their family culture, and Lou's company were all at risk for the same fundamental reason—because of the same issue that lies at the heart of all conflicts in the world, even the biggest conflict of all, centered in the Middle East. It turns out that people in conflict value something else more highly than they value solutions. *The Anatomy of Peace* shows what this is and demonstrates how conflicts at home, conflicts at work, and conflicts in the world stem from the same root cause. Furthermore, the book shows how we systematically misunderstand that cause and unwittingly perpetuate the very problems we think we are trying to solve. The book will launch you on a compelling and multilayered journey of discovery into the foundational cause of conflict, misguided beliefs that perpetuate conflicts, and the way to resolve conflicts large and small.

The Anatomy of Peace has been instrumental in breaking down silos in organizations, transforming law enforcement methodologies and results, providing the framework for whole college conflict curriculums, healing labor-management rifts, and saving marriages and other relationships. Business and governmental leaders, parents, professors, and conflict professionals alike use the book as a guide for finding solutions to their most challenging problems.

Leadership and Self-Deception and *The Anatomy of Peace* help people become aware of a problem they didn't know they had. They equip readers to understand how they can leave the box and engage with others more collaboratively and productively. Arbinger's latest best-seller, *The Outward Mindset*, details how to implement and sustain that change across organizations. Read chapter 1 from *The Outward Mindset*.

1 • A Different Approach

Two black cargo vans snake down Wabash Avenue in Kansas City, Missouri. The passengers are members of the Kansas City Police Department (KCPD) SWAT team. They are about to serve a high-risk drug warrant—the fifth warrant service of that day. The targets of this warrant are sufficiently dangerous that the squad has obtained a "no-knock" warrant, meaning that they will storm through the door unannounced. The men are dressed in black from head to toe, their faces covered by masks that leave only their eyes exposed. Bullet-resistant helmets and body armor make them an intimidating sight.

Senior Sergeant Charles "Chip" Huth, leader of the 1910 SWAT Squad for eight years, is driving the lead van. He slows as the target residence comes into view, and his men stream from both vehicles as quietly and quickly as they can.

Three officers sprint around to the back of the house and take cover, supplying containment should the targets attempt to flee. Seven others, including Chip, run to the front door, six of them with their guns drawn. The seventh runs a well-used battering ram up to the door and slams it through.

"Police," they yell. "Everybody down!" Inside is bedlam. Men attempt to scramble out of the room, some to the stairs and others down hallways. Young children stand as if paralyzed, screaming. A number of women cower in terror on the floor, some of them shielding infants who are screaming at the top of their lungs.

Two of the men—the two suspects, it turns out—go for their weapons but are taken down by officers. "Don't even think about it!" the officers shout. Then they pull the men's arms behind them and put them in cuffs.

With all the young children, the scene in this home is more hectic than most, but within five minutes, the two suspects lie facedown on the living-room floor, and the rest of the inhabitants have been gathered into the dining room.

With everyone's safety secured, the officers begin their search. They move with purpose and precision. Chip notices his point man, Bob Evans, leaving the room, and he assumes Bob is simply joining the search.

A couple of minutes later, Chip passes the kitchen as he walks down the hall. Bob is standing at the kitchen sink. A moment earlier, Bob had been rifling through the kitchen cabinets looking for white powder—not for contraband to be used as evidence against those they are arresting but for a white powder that was of much greater immediate importance. He was looking for Similac. With babies crying and their mothers understandably in hysterics, this most alpha male of all the alpha males on Chip's squad was looking for a way to help them. When Chip sees him, Bob is mixing baby bottles.

Bob looks at Chip with a faint smile and shrugs. He then picks up the bottles and begins distributing them to the mothers of the crying infants. Chip is delighted by this. He hadn't thought of baby bottles himself, but he completely understands what Bob is up to and why.

This one act of responsiveness changed the entire scene. Everyone calmed down, and Chip and his men were able to explain the situation thoroughly and then smoothly turn the two suspects over to the detectives. Nevertheless, mixing baby bottles was such an unusual and unpredictable act that many people in police work—including the members of this SWAT team just a few years earlier—would have considered it irrational. But in Chip's squad, this kind of responsiveness is routine.

It wasn't always this way. To appreciate the remarkable transformation that had come to the 1910 SWAT Squad, we need to learn a little of Chip's challenging background and his history in the Kansas City Police Department.

Chip was born in 1970, the son of an alcoholic, abusive career criminal and a bipolar, schizophrenic mother. When Chip's father was around, the family usually was running from the law—moving from state to state around the South. When his father was absent, Chip, his siblings, and their mother often lived out of a car, collecting cans and cardboard for recycling as a way to survive.

One time when his father returned, promising that things would be different, his abuse of the family escalated. Chip, age ten at the time, stood up to him, and this finally prompted Chip's mother to call the one person her husband feared— her ex–Special Forces brother, who came to wrest the family away from the man. "I'm here to get my sister and the kids," he told Chip's father. "If you get up off that couch, it's going to be the last thing you ever do." That was the last time Chip saw his father.

Chip's father hated cops, which is the primary reason Chip became one. He joined KCPD in 1992. After three years as a patrol officer, he was moved to a SWAT team. Four years later, he joined the police academy as a use-of-force and firearms instructor. He was promoted to SWAT sergeant in 2004. The chief of police thought that the 1910 and 1920 SWAT Squads, which act as the strong arm of the Investigations Bureau of the police department, were out of control. Chip came in as a hatchet man to fix them.

What the chief may not have known, however, was that at the time, Chip was psychologically better suited to *lead* such a group than he was to change it. He made sure to out-work all his men so that he could kick their butts if necessary. Whenever he felt threatened, he responded with threats of violence, and he was just unstable enough that his team members were kept in line.

He was even more severe with the public. The way he saw things, there really are bad guys in the world (he should know since he grew up with one), and they need to be dealt with in a way that makes them sorry they ever committed a crime. Everyone the team members arrested, they took down *hard*. And they didn't much care how they treated people's property or pets. It wasn't uncommon for some of Chip's men to spit tobacco on suspects' furniture, for example, or to put a bullet though the skull of a potentially dangerous dog.

Chip's squad was one of the most complained-about units in KCPD. Some of that was to be expected, since SWAT officers tend to do more damage than regular officers on the street. But even so, the rate of complaints against the squad was alarming, and the cost of the associated litigation was a drain on the department. Chip didn't see a problem with this. He believed his squad was working with people in the only way it could. In fact, he thought the more complaints he and his squad received, the more proof they had that they were doing something right!

A couple of years after Chip took over the SWAT squad, another KCPD officer, Jack Colwell, helped Chip see some truths about himself that startled him—about the person Chip had become and how his attitude and methods were actually undercutting his effectiveness and putting his men and their missions at risk. This revelation coincided with a troubling encounter Chip had with his fifteen-year-old son. Driving his son home from school one day, Chip could tell that something was on his mind and began asking question after question of his son, with no response. "Why won't you tell me what's bothering you?" Chip asked. "You wouldn't understand," his son responded. "Why?" Chip asked. Then his son gave Chip the answer that perhaps prepared him to hear what Jack had to say: "Because you're a robot, Dad."

This comment cut deep. Chip began thinking about the kind of person he had become. He had believed that suspicion and aggression were necessary for survival and success in a vicious, combative, and violent world. But now he started to see that being this kind of person did not put a stop to the viciousness and combat; it actually accelerated it.

These events started Chip on a journey of change, an endeavor that resulted in a complete transformation of the work of his squad. The team used to receive two to three complaints a month, many of them regarding excessive use of force. On average, these complaints cost the department $70,000 per incident. However, because of the team members' new way of working, they haven't had a complaint filed against them in six years. It is rare, now, that they leave others' personal property in shambles or shoot a dog. They even hired a dog specialist to teach them ways to control potentially dangerous animals. And they never spit tobacco. Chip told his men, "Unless you can tell me that chewing tobacco in people's homes advances the mission, we're not doing that anymore." And, of course, they prepare baby bottles.

These changes have increased the cooperation Chip and his team receive from suspects and from the community, and the results have been astounding. In addition to shrinking community complaints against them to zero, in the first three years after adopting this approach, the 1910 SWAT Squad recovered more illegal drugs and guns than it had in the previous decade.

What transformed the team's approach and effectiveness? A different kind of mindset than the members ever had before: a way of seeing and thinking that we call an *outward mindset.*

Mark Ballif and Paul Hubbard, co-CEOs of a highly respected healthcare company, have built their organization utilizing an outward-mindset approach similar to the one Chip has used with his squad. A few years ago, they were meeting with the principals of a venerable private equity firm in New York City. With 32 percent and 30 percent compound annual growth rates in top-line revenue and profitability, respectively, over the prior five years, getting meetings like this one with potential capital investors hadn't been difficult for Mark and Paul.

"So you have turned around over fifty healthcare facilities?" the firm's managing partner asked.

Mark and Paul nodded.

"How?"

Mark and Paul looked at each other, waiting for the other to answer. "It all hinges on finding and developing the right leaders," Mark finally said.

"And what is the most important qualification you look for in a leader?" Mark and Paul felt as if they were being cross-examined.

"Humility," Paul answered. "That's what distinguishes those who can turn these facilities around from those who can't. Leaders who succeed are those who are humble enough to be able to see beyond themselves and perceive the true capacities and capabilities of their people. They don't pretend to have all the answers. Rather, they create an environment that encourages their people to take on the primary responsibility for finding answers to the challenges they and their facilities face."

The other members of the equity firm in the meeting looked at the managing partner, who sat poker-faced.

"Humility?" he finally said, his tone condescending. "You're telling me that you've acquired fifty failing facilities and turned each of them around by finding leaders who have *humility?*"

"Yes," Mark and Paul replied without hesitation.

The managing partner stared at them for a moment. Then he pushed his chair back from the table and rose to his feet. "That doesn't compute to me." With little more than a handshake, he turned and strode out of the room, leaving behind a compelling investment opportunity in a company with a proven track record. What he couldn't comprehend was how the company's results depended on humble leaders who "see beyond themselves," as Paul had described.

Nearly fifteen years earlier, Mark, Paul, and another early partner decided to try their hand at building their own company. They had less than ten years of experience in healthcare between them, but they saw an opportunity to create a unique organization in an industry plagued with problems. So they began purchasing the clinically and financially beleaguered facilities their competitors were desperate to be rid of. They were convinced that the key missing ingredient in failing healthcare operations was not an absence of the right people or even the right location but an absence of the right mindset. They engaged in a systematic approach to apply the principles that are presented in this book.

Mark explains their experience this way: "Some of our competition couldn't get rid of facilities and their teams fast enough because they thought that the teams were simply defective. Our thesis was that we could take a poorly led and therefore underperforming facility and, by helping the existing team see what was possible, *they* could turn it around."

As they acquired their first facilities, they encountered a pattern that would repeat itself, almost without exception, acquisition after acquisition. The outgoing leader, trying to do them a favor, would give them a list of the five or so staff members they would need to fire if they stood any chance of turning things around. "We would thank them for the list and then go to work," Paul and Mark reminisced. "Invariably, four of the five people would turn out to be our best performers."

Consider what this demonstrates. If those who had been identified as problems could, when working under new leadership and a new approach, become star performers, then organizational improvement, even turnaround, is less a matter of getting the wrong people off the bus than a matter of helping people see. It is a matter of changing mindset.

"Leaders fail," Paul explains, "by coming in saying, 'Here's the vision. Now you go execute what I see.' That's just wrong in our view of the world." Continuing, he says, "Although leaders should provide a mission or context and point toward what is possible, what humble, good leaders *also* do is to help people see. When people see, they are able to exercise all their human agency and initiative. When they do that, they own their work. When people are free to execute what they see, rather than simply to enact the instructions of the leader, they can change course in the moment to respond to ever-changing, situation-specific needs. That kind of nimbleness and responsiveness is something you can't manage, force, or orchestrate."

Mark and Paul learned these lessons early on as they operated their first few facilities themselves. Reading situations attentively, they found themselves mixing plenty of baby bottles—taking responsibility to do whatever each situation required. As they acquired more facilities, they needed other leaders who could operate with an outward mindset—people who would mix baby bottles as necessary and help others learn to do the same.

This book is about how to help unlock this kind of collaboration, innovation, and responsiveness—how to experience a way of seeing, thinking, working, and leading that helps individuals, teams, and organizations significantly improve performance.

At first, you might feel like the private equity firm leader who walked out of the meeting with Mark and Paul. The ideas we will cover may not make perfect sense to you early on, and you might wonder whether these concepts can help you with the challenges you are currently facing. We invite you to stay in the meeting. You will learn an actionable, repeatable, and scalable way to transform your personal, team, and organizational performance.

Just as importantly, you will begin seeing situations outside of work differently as well. You will see new and better ways to interact with those you care most about, including those you find most difficult. Everything in this book that applies to people in organizations applies to people in their home and family lives as well—and vice versa. This is why we include corporate, home, and individual stories. Lessons learned from each will apply across the board.

Our journey begins with an idea that Chip, Mark, and Paul believe to be foundational: *mindset drives and shapes all that we do—how we engage with others and how we behave in every moment and situation.*

Index

About the Arbinger Institute

The Arbinger Institute delivers training, consulting, coaching, and digital tools to help individuals and organizations change mindset, transform culture, accelerate collaboration and innovation, resolve conflict, and sustainably improve results.

Arbinger introduced its ideas to a worldwide readership with its first book, *Leadership and Self-Deception*, in 2000. The book is a word-of-mouth phenomenon that has been translated into over 30 languages. This was followed by a second international bestseller, *The Anatomy of Peace*, in 2006, which presents Arbinger's unique approach to conflict resolution and personal growth. *The Outward Mindset*, published in 2016, details how to move individuals, teams, and organizations from in-the-box, inward-mindset orientations to out-of-the-box, outward-mindset orientations.

As a result of its 35-year track record with clients, Arbinger is now recognized as a world leader in the areas of mindset change, leadership, team building, conflict resolution, strategy, and culture change. Arbinger's clients range from individuals who are seeking help in their lives to many of the largest companies and governmental institutions in the world.

Worldwide interest in Arbinger's work has propelled the growth of Arbinger across the globe. Headquartered in the United States, Arbinger now has offices in nearly 30 countries, including throughout the Americas, Europe, Africa, the Middle East, India, Oceania, and Asia.

Arbinger's Mission and Process

The Arbinger Institute's mission is to turn the world outward — to help individuals, teams, and organizations get out of the box and become more connected, aware, and attentive to the needs, objectives, and challenges of colleagues, neighbors, family members, and even rivals. We work with organizations both large and small, well known and out of the spotlight, helping them become, in their respective marketplaces, the equivalent of Zagrum Company in its marketplace.

In our work with clients, we follow a five-step process: (1) assess, (2) train, (3) implement, (4) reassess, and (5) sustain. Before engaging, we assess organizational performance to get a baseline from which to determine best courses of action and against which to measure client progress. To get this baseline, we utilize key organizational metrics and administer the Arbinger Mindset Assessment instrument. We then educate employees by equipping them through training with the following sets of outward-mindset implementation tools: self-awareness tools, mindset-change tools, accountability tools, collaboration tools, and (for managers) leadership tools. These tools set up an implementation game plan that we then help leaders and team members enact. We track progress and adjust the implementation game plan by conducting reassessments at regular intervals. We sustain progress by building up internal expertise and helping organizational leaders turn systems and processes outward so that they incentivize and reward outward-mindset working rather than inward-mindset working. This work ranges from strategic planning to systems reengineering to mentoring and executive coaching.

Sustained growth cannot come from expertise and that resides outside an organization. While short-term growth sometimes can be purchased that way, ongoing sustained growth cannot be outsourced. An organization will rise only as far as its own people are equipped to take it. For these reasons, Arbinger's aim is to position and equip our clients with enough understanding of and expertise in Arbinger's outward-mindset tools and processes to be able to "consult themselves" over time.

Arbinger embeds its expertise within client organizations in part by preparing and certifying internal experts to deliver Arbinger programs within their organizations. To learn more about Arbinger's training and consulting services, find out how to become an Arbinger facilitator within your organization, or explore other Arbinger publications and access client case studies, please visit www.arbinger .com or contact us by phone at our US headquarters at 801-447-9244.

ALSO BY THE ARBINGER INSTITUTE

THE OUTWARD MINDSET

Seeing Beyond Ourselves | How to Change Lives and Transform Organizations

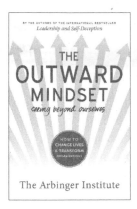

"The secret to teamwork is an outward mindset. This is the definitive guide on how to achieve it."
—Steve Young, two-time NFL MVP and Hall-of-Fame Quarterback

"A must-read for leaders seeking significant and lasting organizational change."
—John Wilson, President, International Operations, Staples

"A powerful book with a powerful message about really seeing. It opens a path to trust, collaboration, creativity, and performance."
—Katherine Klein, Professor of Management, Wharton School

With unique grace and clarity, this book describes the one change that can dramatically improve organizational performance, spark innovation, strengthen all your relationships, and make your life and the lives of everyone around you better. The key is to change how you see and relate to the world. Changing from a self-focused inward mindset to an others-inclusive outward mindset makes a dramatic difference in results, satisfaction, and engagement. *The Outward Mindset* presents compelling true stories and simple yet profound guidance and tools to help individuals, teams, and organizations move from inward-mindset orientations to outward-mindset orientations.

Leaders who serve others with an outward mindset encourage a culture of collaboration where everybody wins. Read *The Outward Mindset* and learn how great servant leaders think.

—Ken Blanchard, coauthor of *The New One Minute Manager®*

Paperback, 192 pages, ISBN 978-1-62656-715-3
PDF ebook ISBN 978-1-62656-716-0
Digital audio ISBN 978-1-62656-719-1
800.929.2929

Berrett-Koehler Publishers, Inc.
bkconnection.com

BK

Berrett–Koehler
Publishers

Berrett-Koehler is an independent publisher dedicated to an ambitious mission: *Connecting people and ideas to create a world that works for all.*

We believe that the solutions to the world's problems will come from all of us, working at all levels: in our organizations, in our society, and in our own lives. Our BK Business books help people make their organizations more humane, democratic, diverse, and effective (we don't think there's any contradiction there). Our BK Currents books offer pathways to creating a more just, equitable, and sustainable society. Our BK Life books help people create positive change in their lives and align their personal practices with their aspirations for a better world.

All of our books are designed to bring people seeking positive change together around the ideas that empower them to see and shape the world in a new way.

And we strive to practice what we preach. At the core of our approach is Stewardship, a deep sense of responsibility to administer the company for the benefit of all of our stakeholder groups including authors, customers, employees, investors, service providers, and the communities and environment around us. Everything we do is built around this and our other key values of quality, partnership, inclusion, and sustainability.

This is why we are both a B-Corporation and a California Benefit Corporation—a certification and a for-profit legal status that require us to adhere to the highest standards for corporate, social, and environmental performance.

We are grateful to our readers, authors, and other friends of the company who consider themselves to be part of the BK Community. We hope that you, too, will join us in our mission.

A BK Business Book

We hope you enjoy this BK Business book. BK Business books pioneer new leadership and management practices and socially responsible approaches to business. They are designed to provide you with groundbreaking and practical tools to transform your work and organizations while upholding the triple bottom line of people, planet, and profits. High-five!

To find out more, visit **www.bkconnection.com**.

Berrett–Koehler
Publishers

Connecting people and ideas
to create a world that works for all

Dear Reader,

Thank you for picking up this book and joining our worldwide community of Berrett-Koehler readers. We share ideas that bring positive change into people's lives, organizations, and society.

To welcome you, we'd like to offer you a free e-book. You can pick from among twelve of our bestselling books by entering the promotional code BKP92E here: http://www.bkconnection.com/welcome.

When you claim your free e-book, we'll also send you a copy of our e-newsletter, the *BK Communiqué*. Although you're free to unsubscribe, there are many benefits to sticking around. In every issue of our newsletter you'll find

• A free e-book
• Tips from famous authors
• Discounts on spotlight titles
• Hilarious insider publishing news
• A chance to win a prize for answering a riddle

Best of all, our readers tell us, "Your newsletter is the only one I actually read." So claim your gift today, and please stay in touch!

Sincerely,

Charlotte Ashlock
Steward of the BK Website

Questions? Comments? Contact me at bkcommunity@bkpub.com.

MIX
Paper from
responsible sources
FSC® C016245
www.fsc.org

Certified
Corporation
bcorporation.net